Growing EXCEPTIONAL SEEDLINGS

Companionship for Parents of Neurodivergent Kids

KENDRA ROGERS

Copyright © 2020 Kendra Rogers.

All rights reserved. No part of this book may be used or reproduced by any means, graphic, electronic, or mechanical, including photocopying, recording, taping or by any information storage retrieval system without the written permission of the author except in the case of brief quotations embodied in critical articles and reviews.

This book is a work of non-fiction. Unless otherwise noted, the author and the publisher make no explicit guarantees as to the accuracy of the information contained in this book and in some cases, names of people and places have been altered to protect their privacy.

Archway Publishing books may be ordered through booksellers or by contacting:

Archway Publishing
1663 Liberty Drive
Bloomington, IN 47403
www.archwaypublishing.com
1 (888) 242-5904

Because of the dynamic nature of the Internet, any web addresses or links contained in this book may have changed since publication and may no longer be valid. The views expressed in this work are solely those of the author and do not necessarily reflect the views of the publisher, and the publisher hereby disclaims any responsibility for them.

Any people depicted in stock imagery provided by Getty Images are models, and such images are being used for illustrative purposes only. Certain stock imagery © Getty Images.

ISBN: 978-1-4808-9229-3 (sc)
ISBN: 978-1-4808-9228-6 (hc)
ISBN: 978-1-4808-9230-9 (e)

Library of Congress Control Number: 2020913338

Print information available on the last page.

Archway Publishing rev. date: 08/20/2020

Dedicated to my family and my tribe. I couldn't have done this without you all!

To my husband, Leigh. You have supported me through this endeavor. I couldn't have completed this without your encouragement. I love you always.

To my son Will. Without your inspiration, I wouldn't have even thought to write this book. Thank you for being the shining beacon of love that you are.

Special thanks to Kendra Wysocki, whose agreement to cooperate with me in this endeavor spurred me to actually complete it. And who reminded me about all the sensory struggles our glorious children overcome daily!

Contents

Introduction ix
    What Is Neurodiversity? xi
    Comorbidities xii

Chapter 1
    Labels 1
    Diagnostic Grief 4
    Early Signs/Symptoms 7
    Sensory Component 11

Chapter 2
    Coping Strategies, Therapies, and Medications 14

Chapter 3
    Progress and Regression 26
    Sleep 29
    Brain development 31

Chapter 4
    Discipline Methods 39

Chapter 5
    Routines 56
    Food 58

Chapter 6
    Parenting Together 63
    Parenting Struggles and Support..68
    Parental Rivalry 74

Chapter 7
    Immediate Family Involvement.. 78
    Siblings..84
    Sibling Differences..87
    Extended Family..92

Chapter 8
    Schooling Options and Accommodations.........................97
    Parent Stories... 105
    Teachers... 113

Chapter 9
    Tough Subjects... 118
    Religion.. 118
    Death 120
    Injustice/World Violence/Events 122
    Sexuality 124

Chapter 10
    Beginners' Guide to Raising Neurodivergent Children... 127
    Life Hacks.. 132

Resources 137
Works Cited 143

Introduction

At only a year old, Johnny drops his arms and head and sobs—heartbroken. Another toddler has just taken his toy. You hug him, wipe his tears away, and acknowledge and name his feelings of sadness and frustration. Then you solve. He's happy again.

At two, George does not have words to adequately express his feelings of frustration when you abruptly tell him to clean up his toys. He throws a typical toddler tantrum. He cannot ask for resolution time for the elaborate game he was playing. He doesn't have the language. You scoop him up and make him clean up, though you acknowledge cleaning is no fun and you hear his anger.

At three, James is in his own world and doesn't hear your calls for his attention. When you forcibly gain his focus by getting in between him and his toys, he screams at you. You think he is rude and disrespectful. You tell him as much. He can't communicate that you interrupted an epic car chase and destroyed his game.

You think your toddler is a typical toddler, but there is so much more going on in his brain than you can imagine or access. He can sign to you but cannot verbalize his complex thoughts. He cannot name his feelings.

Sally, four, screams at Paul, her two-year-old brother, for carelessly knocking a doll out of place. You scold your daughter because she should be able to speak respectfully, but she doesn't have the words to express her mountainous feelings about her game being trampled upon. She cannot tell you every move and thought that went into the story and what her brother's accidental actions caused in her game.

At five, Samantha, now highly verbal and reading, melts down in the store and refuses to leave. You've been there for two hours already and ready for the next thing. She's not though. There was one shelf she needed to look at to have closure about leaving, but she's so overwhelmed with the amount of time passed and the colorful displays that she's unable to express her thoughts in a way you can understand.

You think your preschooler might be a bit more challenging than a typical preschooler, but these incidents are typical of others as well. Sure, your daughter might have multihour meltdowns on a weekly basis, but the crying isn't anything you can't handle.

Tommy, six, rails against your request for him do his school work but cannot articulate why he struggles so much right now. He hasn't told you the schedule is wrong. He hasn't told you he had certain expectations you changed without warning.

Your seven year old, Charlie, challenges his five-year-old brother, James, every time you turn around. You think the fights are plain old sibling rivalry. They aren't. Charlie is challenged by his brother's abilities, which he doesn't share. Sure, he has his own, but he doesn't see those as strengths but as normal. He can't tell you he feels threatened by his brother's physical abilities. He just picks fights and tries to be better and then has meltdowns when his brother won't, or can't, listen and live up to his expectations.

Samuel, eight, still has meltdowns over what seem to be trivial aspects of life like the color of his spoon for snack time. You try every day to help him navigate this harsh world because he's a lover. He's sensitive. You feel like you fail constantly. Other people think he throws fits because he is manipulative. You know better. He can't control himself. You don't yet know why, but you know he can't. Because you were the one trying to change him for all those prior years. You have held him while he sobbed into your chest about his insurmountable feelings. You have cried to your partner about feelings of helplessness. You want to fix the emotions. You breathe. You realize there is nothing to be fixed. This child has anxiety. He isn't broken. He's incredible. He needs help. You need help.

At nine, hormones begin to surge as is typical. And Jason's struggles ramp up again. He is better about articulating his difficulties than he was a year ago. But he still gets angry and overwhelmed. You attend large events as a family and constantly check in with him about how he's feeling. Is he overwhelmed? Is he coping okay? How can we help him? Therapy? Medication? Diet changes? He needs something more than a typical child at his age. His reactions are not typical.

At ten, Will is steadily approaching puberty and a rapid time of change in his life and body. He still experiences meltdowns weekly. He still struggles with flexibility. He still masks his true needs with unrelated feelings. We are approaching the time when kids like Will are very prone to suicide. We work to prevent suicide and raise him to the powerhouse of an adult he is capable of being.

What Is Neurodiversity?

Neurodiversity is simply differences in how our brains work. Neurotypical people function in roughly the same way. They think similarly and learn similarly. Their brains react to information in similar manners too. Being neurodiverse means the brain reacts differently to information. People may process very quickly and crave more information. New facts may take a bit to assimilate, but once their brains do, they crave more or make connections others wouldn't. Some brains need to learn more than one lesson simultaneously. Or need to learn while moving. Some brains miss social cues or are hypervigilant.

Trial and error is the only way we can figure out how to meet each different brain. Tests to determine what neurodivergence is present are subjective, and results vary based on practitioner. Treatment plans also differ based on practitioner and patient. As the parent or caregiver, we know our children best and can help lead the plans. We reserve the right to say no when we're uncomfortable and to push for other treatments or therapies.

Comorbidities

Neurodiversity comes in many varieties. Twice exceptional (2E) applies to those individuals who have two or more deviations from the norm. Diagnoses include ADHD and giftedness or anxiety and ADD or autism and dyslexia. Many of these are considered comorbid which simply means they're likely to occur together. Anxiety and giftedness are comorbid too. Giftedness is sneaky because it often hides behind another diagnosis or two. People, especially schools, see the other diagnoses and don't see higher intelligence goes along.

When people see Mack, my son who struggles with sensory processing disorder, touching everything and struggling to put away a toy because light distracts him, they don't think he is capable of giftedness. He also didn't start reading until he was over seven, and even then, he wasn't great. Being exceptional doesn't mean reading at age two or three. Giftedness can also mean a greater spatial acuity. Or a deeper understanding of physics and chemistry at an early age. The need to move constantly isn't exclusively a focus issue. Constant action is often linked with the brain moving very quickly and calculating several items simultaneously.

People like Mack can look at a problem from several angles

at once and quickly suggest several solutions, many of which even solve the problem. They may be able to accomplish this before others even identify the problem. Understanding people with this skill can also forget how to tie their shoes or turn clothes the correct way before putting them on is a challenge. This difference is called asynchrony. Asynchrony is an interesting way to raise a child. And frustrating. Constant reminders are met with rolled eyes. Suggestions for visual charts are often made, but they don't work. This child doesn't see those reminders unless they flash at him. Mack rode his bike smoothly without training wheels after just two tries at age six but couldn't read or write well, which confuses many. Mack could multiply just by looking at objects at age four but couldn't set the table without the reminder about plates and silverware, which also confounds people.

Those with perceived focus difficulties often are misunderstood. They're seen as undisciplined and random. If you really watch, they have many focuses simultaneously. They miss trivial details like their shoes outside in the rain, but they'll quickly figure out what's wrong with your car and the best way to fix the problem. They're not always mechanical, of course, but they can see solutions to complex problems, while tiny details elude them. Children who struggle thusly are often labeled as troublemakers or unintelligent. They get into a lot of trouble, certainly, but a lot of it comes from a good place. For instance, when the boys tore up a portion of my deck, it was because they were bored but *also* because Mack had heard me discuss the need so he "helped." Raising children like Mack is difficult. They need constant reminders and step-by-step instructions with details. And then, another reminder.

They often struggle with planning things out too. We have to help their executive functions. Deciding what to wear and when to get dressed are far more problematic than for neurotypical people. They can benefit from solid organizational systems and few complicated choices. Cleaning their rooms or putting toys away is completely lost. I often have to point out every item Mack needs to clean in his room. To them, order isn't an issue. Mack wants to build wooden creations. He has his own tools and wood pieces. He has great ideas too. What he lacks is the plan and execution. He wants to build a toy car for Kae for Christmas. I have told him he needs to plan it, measure it, and draw it. He hasn't done so yet. The planning is too much for his brain and to slow to accomplish. Leigh or I will have to help him.

These little (or big) people who struggle to focus are incredible thinkers. Socrates, Dali, Emily Dickinson, the Wright brothers, and so many more incredible contributors to our modern world and arenas of thought were in this group of people who couldn't focus or who struggled with executive function. We think these great minds should have had the ability to plan, document, and focus, but their minds were constantly moving. We make an egregious error to assume one with these difficulties was a troublemaker or incapable of higher order thought processes. Yet Einstein was expelled from school because his intelligence was misunderstood as troublesomeness. Their difficulty focusing is seated either in their minds moving quickly and computing at an incredible rate or their minds being bored and needing to create entertainment or challenge.

When we witness the latter, we can assist with direction or projects for their minds. While with the former, we can provide access to a wealth of resources for their brains to feast on. We need to provide stimulation in their interest areas. You wouldn't give an artistic person a skyscraper to build. Mack needs things he can create and tinker with, but markers and paper result in colorful walls and tiny scraps of paper. He isn't being malicious, though we assume he is. Really, he is conducting experiments. I don't know what sort of experiments involve wall coloring, but I do know if I want him positively occupied, I need to provide proper materials.

And I need to be prepared to help clean up or help him remember how and where to clean up.

I took too long to figure out Mack didn't destroy Will's toys intentionally. He investigated them and learned about them. When he was not yet three and explained to me how his bicycle worked (without taking it apart), I realized his *destruction* wasn't destruction and I entirely shifted my parenting paradigm for him. I was intentional about his toy options—lots of LEGO products, magnets, wooden blocks, toys that should snap together and apart, things he could rearrange, train tracks, and more. He is now eight and has learned, mostly, how to reign in his experiments and how to ask if certain investigation is okay. Mack has learned he has this need too and to foster it is to be happy. We also have the opportunity to work at a large farm several times a week and one of the owners does the building and mechanical repairs. I am thankful this man has not only accepted my son's puppylike trailing but embraced him. He teaches Mack about the electricity, shelters, and engines. Mack is invited to tag along with *the men* and hand them tools and climb ladders. His brain is going miles a minute but when he is working with *the men*, he couldn't be happier or more focused on his tasks. He's learning. All parts of him are actively engaged in the goal and the steps to get there.

People who struggle with focus need to be engaged in multiple ways. They cannot sit still with only their brains engaged. Exclusively working their bodies doesn't help either. They need both. They need cross-hemispheric involvement. Fidget toys can help them focus better on what they would perceive as mundane brain tasks. And on boring ones. These tasks are often necessary parts of life, but for those who struggle in this area, they can be amazingly burdensome. They need something to engage with while they wait too.

They are often either the first to complete an activity or cannot or will not complete the project in the space given. Therefore, they wait. Lingering is a dangerous game for these people. Waiting is how I ended up with a torn-up deck and almost a disassembled bike. Occupying waiting people can be challenging but necessary. Rarely books can help, but often something designed to keep their bodies moving is better. A trampoline, stationary bike, treadmill, or similar device can help when possible. However, space is limited and any of those items in a classroom would prove a challenge. Fidget toys, TheraBand, large exercise balls, or brain teasers for certain people can help and are often workable in a classroom. Long lines can be the most arduous task and the most difficult to remedy. Conversation about what's around the line or about the anticipated activity can help. Asking difficult questions and engaging in conversation they're interested in can also prove successful. We often play "I spy" while in lines. Games engage both sensory and internal needs. Bribes sometimes work for short times but often wear off quickly. Blackmail is never acceptable, but I have witnessed it. Waiting in line or in a waiting room with one of these children can be like trying to capture a fruit fly buzzing around your kitchen.

Specific expectations and doing everything possible to minimize the wait will go furthest to help decrease troublesome behavior, but upsetting someone is inevitable. Whether you, your child, or a bystander, someone may end up frustrated. If you or your child, you can always use some collaborative problem-solving to determine and address the issue for next time. If a bystander is upset when your child acts like a child, there are a few options (not many will work out well), but mostly ignore them if possible. And remember your precious child is precocious. Pinning them down while waiting simply isn't possible. Nor would the attempt result in anyone being happy.

Mack has struggled lately with maintaining control of his body and mouth. I remind him often he needs to reign in and take control of his body. I nag really. I hate it. He hates it. He doesn't change. He's also been whiny, which isn't his typical disposition. And there have been lots of *I wish* types of statements, which I am trying desperately to quell. He's leaping. I am certain of it. Something *big* is happening in his brain. Bigger than normal. He's struggling. He needs more vestibular and proprioceptive input. He needs squeezes, running, and jumping. He needs to touch things and talk.

I need to give him opportunities for those outlets and inputs rather than attempt to squelch his clearly developing brain. I am weary though. I am tired of telling him to stop in the car because I cannot handle the noises. (I am an avoider. He is a seeker.) I am worn out from the constant demand for him to chill. He gets loads of activity every day. Physical activity. But we have been busy, so we haven't been challenging the cognitive channels as much. I need to fix that. I need to ensure *both* types of input are occurring. Physical health is important, but fostering mental acuity and growth is too. This can be challenging given he cannot sit still long enough to read an entire level one reader book with fewer than one hundred words. We must move while we learn. Coloring or writing isn't enough. He needs whole body movement and different perspectives like upside down to achieve the sort of focus he needs. Meeting all Mack's needs all the time is hard but pays off.

Anxiety is another common struggle for people with 2E. Extreme fear about a typically dangerous experience like snakes or death is often misconstrued for anxiety. While these situations can absolutely be part of the disquiet, they are not all encompassing. Anxiety causes several uncontrollable reactions, which include racing heartbeat, increased respirations, sweatiness, nausea, distortions of reality, and thoughts of rage. Anxiety produces fight-or-flight hormones in the body and a person must choose without thought what to do to preserve life, even though their lives are not in danger. Frustration at incomplete tasks and the need to adjust for changes in the plan can also produce anxiety.

A person who experiences an anxiety attack or even a moment of heightened anxiety without a full-blown attack may be unable to reach the logical portion of their brains—the frontal cortex—as the amygdala (the emotional center) has taken over operations and the person is now acting on instinct to preserve themselves. Coping mechanisms specific to the individual's needs are crucial in supporting them and regaining their logical selves so they can reach a solution.

Meditating, reading, karate, musical engagement, and grounding are all techniques people with anxiety use to regain control. Meditating helps clear the mind of fearful thoughts. Reading transports people to new, less concerning places. Karate and music are rhythmic and methodical, helping achieve rationality. Grounding involves touching tangible objects to tell the brain there isn't real danger.

Some people experience anxiety in seemingly calm ways. They may withdraw or seem to fade away. Others may explode like Mount Vesuvius into hours-long fits of screams and cries. Others may have fits of rage or violence. They all experience intense feelings and really don't know what to do with them. As caregivers, we can support their need to express those big feelings and give them a safe space to do so. The enormous emotions are overwhelming for them, and support can help the feelings seem less so.

When people feel overcome, they may not be capable of communicating in a way others would understand. Instead, we need to look at their body language and try to assess what will best bring them back to a logical headspace. Filling the logical need also looks different to everyone. Some may need physical activity to express then move past their feelings, and then they have the ability to verbalize. Others may need to scream then be alone to read, journal, or meditate. Still others may harm themselves unintentionally because their anxiety is so high, but they don't or can't feel safe to express their feelings. This bottling and self-harm can become very dangerous. They might look like nervous habits as well but are far more. Numerous potential reactions to anxiety mean we may struggle to identify every one, but recognizing your child can express fretfulness in different ways is crucial to identifying triggers and signs for *your* child. Like with responses to disquiet, the coping mechanisms can be as varied as the number of people on the planet and can change with age, maturity, and understanding.

Stick with what works until it doesn't, then try something new. Flexibility on the part of the caregiver is crucial. Once the mountainous feelings have subsided and the person is back in a safe zone of manageable emotions, discussion about what set off the struggle may be possible. But time to process is still necessary even after the tumultuous experience is past. We can create the kind of relationship in which the person can begin to cope and learn to self-moderate when we demonstrate our ability to be there and wait for the storm to pass. Solutions can only be reached once a person is able to identify and name their feelings, what caused the anxiety attack, and return to a safe mind space.

Sometimes we can stumble upon methods that bring our anxious loved ones out of an attack. For Will, my mispronunciation of dinosaur names caused him to laugh and roll his eyes, thus reminding him he was in a safe space. The next time I attempted this trick, I failed. I haven't accidentally found another subtle trick yet.

Will responds best if he's given a break and told we are ready to talk when he is. We aren't able to reach him while he's melting down. Some answer to silliness like the dinosaur mispronunciation. Others can be pulled into logic with a certain calming song. Others might respond to math facts rapid fire. Still others may benefit from a physical challenge to reset. You can try anything and everything your child might respond to. And continue to try until you find the key for your child.

Not everyone recognizes anxiety is real, however. And when the condition goes undiagnosed and untreated, life can go very badly. Those who struggle with undiagnosed and untreated anxiety or other mental differences perpetrate more harm against themselves and others than other group. A site (https://www.ncbi.nlm.nih.gov/pmc/articles/PMC2686644/) discusses the increase in self-harm among those with mental differences. Seeking professional help is crucial, even with milder cases.

Even when people recognize anxiety is real, they often dismiss it. Particularly if the symptoms don't look a certain way. This can result in a lack of treatment. Anxiety doesn't present identically in every case. Sometimes extreme fear about a particular element of one's world paralyzes, but not always. An extreme need for control and predictability can also be indicators of a problem. This doesn't mean fear of change as people often perceive. Ignoring these characteristics that deviate from the standard is to ignore anxiety.

Along with disregarding the deviations from the norm, sometimes people lump everyone together with phrases like "Everyone has something different." While this might be true, someone else's different is unique to them and your child's different is also unique. Recognizing an individual is having trouble and helping them is important. Diminishing the distress diminishes the person as well.

"Can you fix it?" I was recently asked this question regarding medication and Will. My immediate response was "He's not broken." The asker questioned innocently enough. She worded her inquiry poorly but really wanted to know if medications could help my son regulate better. I simply told her we weren't to meds at this point. Medication is a valid and often necessary option for kids with anxiety, autism, ADHD, depression, ODD, and a host of other diagnoses. We just aren't there with Will. If you are there with your child, medication still doesn't mean your child is broken or needs fixing but that your child succeeds better with a prescription. Your child is getting the help they need to function in a society that is highly demanding. Therapy and support are enough for Will right now. We want to foster his deep feelings and help him learn to work with who he is in a society not capable of understanding him.

We don't want to fix him. I would rather the world change so he'd be seen as I see him. I see a loving, warm-hearted, fun, musical, strong, little boy with an incredible laugh and gorgeous long, blond hair. I see a horse lover who has an insatiable zest for life and love. I see a paleontologist who knows more about dinosaurs than I ever thought was possible. And a boy who reads constantly and loves getting lost in different worlds. The world sees a boy with a scowl and clenched fists. A boy who blows up when he doesn't get his way. A boy who is manipulative and spoiled. I know better. He knows better. His father knows better. He's misunderstood and struggling. He doesn't need fixing. He's not broken. He feels and thinks deeply, and he needs love and understanding.

Diagnosis can be tricky. A child's primary doctor might suggest seeing a behavioral specialist or a counselor due to red flags you have mentioned or they have witnessed. You might ask for a referral due to concerns you have. In either case, talking to someone about your child's differences won't hurt. Even if your child doesn't struggle with anxiety, seeking out help for difficulty with behavior or emotions can only help. Anxiety diagnoses can be a challenge, particularly in children. They don't tend to exhibit the same signs as adults or even as each other. Silence and seclusion might be anxiety rather than depression. Rage can be anxiety too. Self-harm, harming others, screaming, inflexibility, perfectionism, OCD-like traits, and more can all be manifestations of anxiety. If your child exhibits anything outside what you feel is typical, please seek help. It might well be a variation of normal but catching things early and treating them, even with therapy, can be life-changing in the long run.

The mind is a wild, inventive, sometimes scary place. We understand quite little about it, really. The neural network and processes are largely mystery. Even with modern tools like CT scans and MRIs, we don't understand the way the brain works. We can speculate about what might be going on based on what areas of the brain we have mapped and understand at least a bit about, but even those conjectures are based on theories of how a small percentage of the brain functions. The mind controls the body, but nothing controls the mind. Thoughts and ideas crop up without warning, and we can do little to change or dismiss them. Sometimes we even have to move through these uncontrolled thoughts to access reality. This is part of anxiety. The brain is essentially playing tricks on us. We see reality, but our brains add to or subtract from it. People with anxiety often create problems not fully grounded in reality. They have to shuffle through those invented scenarios to find what they should react to and then decide how to react.

The therapies and medications offered to those struggling with anxiety help them sift through the forests of their brains. They help achieve clarity in storms. Medications work at blocking or enhancing different areas of the brain for optimal function. Therapies teach people how to navigate their brains differently. Neurotypical people don't have to sift through a vat of confusion to access the ability to walk through dead trees. Someone with anxiety, like Will, has to overcome the unfounded fear those dormant trees will reach out and grab him. In reality and in his mind, Will has to overcome these fears just to get through his school day interacting with his siblings.

Notes

Chapter 1

Labels

Labels, or diagnoses, can be a hot topic. Some people believe labeling children or adult affects their lives negatively. They believe it puts people into boxes and ignores their strengths while highlighting their weaknesses. Others believe a diagnosis leads to clearer understanding and research paths. Also, a diagnosis can help identify potential weaknesses that can then be strengthened, due to a more complete understanding. Regardless of where you may fall on this continuum, understanding your child is paramount.

Understanding who my kids are has been one of my biggest goals in parenting. I wanted to do so without outside influences, but the truth is I needed to know what was going on underneath to cause the behaviors I was seeing. I have also been able to direct my research about how to help my children as a result of their diagnoses. Without my road map, I would feel more lost than I do. I resisted for far too long. When Will was not yet two, friends who observed his peculiar play often asked whether he had autism. I always said he was quirky but *normal*. I didn't seek a diagnosis until he was seven and still had explosive meltdowns regularly. Had I listened to the people who questioned his behavior, I might not have exhausted so many discipline and teaching methods before arriving at what works. I might not have beaten myself up over my inability to prevent his feelings from overwhelming him.

Dwelling on the might-haves isn't helpful to me now. I know now. I am doing better. There are times I wish I had known earlier and had addressed Will differently. What matters is how I address him now. I fail now too, but I know what I should be doing and how I ought to be addressing him. I teach those who come in contact with him how to react to him and what his needs are. I teach him, with the help of a therapist, how to cope with his mental differences in a society that doesn't understand him. I know I need to be gentle but direct. Caring but exact with my words. I know he needs all the hugs he asks for and more.

A diagnosis may be necessary for school accommodations too. While this may not be where you want to be, a definition may be needed to get your child the services he or she needs in school settings. Playing along with the system is sometimes a necessary evil. Using the structure of our society to understand and help our children will result in their ability to thrive. If we can understand their brains more fully, we can help them cope with life. Not change who they are to fit the mold but cope with the struggles they will encounter as a result of their differences. As we can't make short people taller, we can't change how our children's brains function. But we can give them tools to help them reach the heights they can achieve.

But fighting the system to get what your child needs may also be necessary. Sometimes a diagnosis is mild, and a school may not agree that modifications are warranted because grades aren't suffering. Knowing that schools are legally required to assess students for suspected learning differences *and* make adjustments so students have what they need to succeed is important. The laws call for the "least restrictive environment possible" for addressing the needs of each student. This means wheelchair ramps so students have access to all areas of the building. Adaptive software and devices for those with reading challenges. Paraprofessionals for those who need one-on-one assistance. And dictation and extra time on tests for those who struggle with information processing.

Fighting the system to get your child's diagnosis is one of the biggest challenges you may face. I had the luxury of time to gain assessments for Will. Many don't because of children engaging in self-harm. Unfortunately, these parents have few options. A friend of mine is experiencing this challenge now. Her daughter has suicidal thoughts (no attempts), and she is trying to get a diagnosis, services, and medications appropriate for the identified struggle. Her options are to wait in line for months for assessment and treatment while her daughter suffers. Or put her daughter in an in-patient hospital where they'd only see each other for one hour a day. If Dee puts Mary in the hospital, a psychiatrist will see her within twenty-four hours. But Dee and her husband, Jim, will have no access or say over what happens with their daughter until she is released to them with whatever diagnosis and medication plan the doctor sees fit. Whether it fits with their beliefs or lifestyle or not, Dee, Jim, and Mary will have to live with whatever someone who's only known them for a brief time decides.

Dee is fighting a broken system to gain the appropriate diagnosis and treatment plan for Mary. The fight may just save Mary's life and is worth tackling. Insurance, location, psychiatrist availability, and child severity all affect the kind of fight you will face. Mine is finding a practitioner close by who takes our insurance and is a good match with Will and our family's values. Yours might include someone with fast availability and a sliding pay scale for deductibles. You might be fighting with Medicaid, as I once did, for services for your child. Often the practitioners are on your side. Use them and their expertise to find the offices and insurance plans that work. The Autism Alliance of Michigan has helped me find additional practitioners as well. More than likely, there are resources like them in your area too. Whatever fight you must engage in to understand your child and provide him or her with the necessary services in the least restrictive environment, do it. You might just save your child's life.

Diagnostic Grief

Grief. It's tricky. People experience many kinds of grief but often only acknowledge certain ones. The death of a loved one and separation from loved ones for other reasons are two very big purveyors of grief. Loss of material goods and pets are as well. A mental health diagnosis is rarely recognized as a reason for grief, however. And we rarely allow our emotions surrounding the diagnosis to be expressed as grief. However, heartbreak is a real, powerful, and appropriate reaction to a health diagnosis. Mental or otherwise.

Others tell me frequently I should be glad for my living children, and I am. But they say I have healthy children who are physically fine and mentally *not that bad*. They say grieving is for mothers who have lost children—a grief I have also experienced four times. They say grief is for mothers whose children can't walk, talk, run, or play with others. They say grief is for mothers who will certainly bury children after too short lives. They say grief isn't for the loss of status quo. I disagree. All our feelings of grief and sadness are valid. So go ahead. Grieve the loss of playground mud and holey jeans; our kids won't wear jeans and get dirty. Feel what you feel, and don't let anyone tell you how.

We have ideals set up and preconceived notions about what parenting will be. We see happy times and, sure, some struggles. But we don't see, or realize, the heartbreak along with something outside *normal*. Normal is what everyone wants. We constantly ask our parents and our friends who were parents before us and our physicians whether things we're seeing are *normal*. When they're not, we strive to find or create normal. Rather than mourn and grieve the loss of the ideal, we attempt to find perfection. Instead, we can grieve the loss of normal and allow ourselves to rejoice in *our* normal. The result is a better outcome for us and our children. Before the rejoicing and embracing of the neurodiversity our children represent, we must let go of the preconceived ideas of what we expected or wanted. To let go, we must grieve.

Grieving the loss of a child who sits in front of you seems harsh, but to acknowledge that child as he or she truly is, we must release the old ideas. We must breathe, release, cry, and move forward. Moving forward with love and a new understanding will result in better futures for you and your child. They will see you recognize them for their true selves and not as some yearned version. You will begin to help them through their struggles rather than try to fix them and their version of the world. You will both begin to empower each other to teach the world about the incredible microcosm you're a small part of.

Empowerment tends to be contagious and begins to catch and spread. Others will see how lovely the uniqueness is and begin to embrace it.

I still sometimes grieve the loss of the children I expected to be normal. I know my son will struggle with relationships, romantic and otherwise. I know he will not be able to interact with most of the world in a meaningful way. Interaction is important to me but might not be to him. Leigh would rather mingle only with those special people he's invited into his bubble. Will is a lot like him. Leigh acquiesces to socializing with my friends when the families are together, but he would be happy not doing so. I suspect my son will be this way too. I need to embrace the happiness my son chooses and not project my own needs onto him.

I grieve also for the lack of normalcy my son Mack experiences daily. He wears a medical alert bracelet, which he often has to explain to peers. He has only ever eaten at home or one of three restaurants. He has only been to one ice cream parlor. When he was a toddler, his older siblings were discussing the candies they loved as they saw them at the toy store. Mack's huge eyes begged me for some shred of normalcy in that moment. And I, though I rarely give my kids candy, bawled like a baby and frantically searched for safe candy for Mack. I knew I was irrational, but we will do whatever we can to give our kids what we feel should be normal.

I grieve the loss of my oldest daughter's playful childhood. Rory can play like a *normal* child but doesn't. Her games have always been too complicated for the playground. She has always played with her brothers or read because the other kids couldn't keep up with her and she was bored with them. She has a few great friends now with whom she can be herself. They know she is peculiar, but they embrace her.

My children will never experience life in the way society calls normal. Most days, I am at peace. There are days when I see kids running and playing tag together without quibbling and I grieve. I grieve when I see other mothers easily exit parks and stores without having had to explain everything their children saw. I grieve when parents don't have to ensure their children have escape techniques for when the gathering is too overwhelming. I rejoice when I see my children loving the lives they have and loving who they are as people. And I truly enjoy who my children are as people. Even when they drive me mad many days.

Early Signs/Symptoms

Food aversions, extreme attachments to people or objects, fussiness about clothing, and extreme reactions to sounds and lights can all indicate something is different about your young child. If you observe other children and notice striking differences in your own, a doctor consultation is in order. Simply addressing your concerns with your child's pediatrician can lead to a referral for a developmental pediatrician who can assess and determine whether there is cause for further investigation and diagnosis. Had I taken Will to the doctor when he was two because of the peculiarities that friends noted, I would have had his autism diagnosis earlier and been able to begin teaching him according to how his brain worked. Don't hesitate to ask the questions. Keep asking if you have concerns. Don't let doctors brush you off when you know something is different.

Noticing neurodiversity in young children is challenging if they're relatively *normal*. If their differences are not striking, we might ignore them as within normal ranges. As they get older, the gaps likely become more evident. Unfortunately, addressing challenges becomes more difficult as children age. Convincing a teen or adult they may need therapy for a mental disorder is far more challenging than taking a young child to therapy. Older people will also struggle to be open about his or her difficulties. But is my screaming toddler really struggling with anxiety? Or are they just a bit extra? Either could be true. But if you're concerned, there is no harm in asking a medical practitioner for advice and input. There could be harm in waiting until things are more obvious.

I often find myself wishing I had asked about my son earlier. As a toddler, he was very attached to me and his home. Everything had a place too. If something was out of order, he would melt down. He was also strongly attached to routines. If things were awry or different in any way, he would melt down. He was far more particular about his clothing, bedding, shoes, socks, etc. than typical toddlers too. Things had to be just so. No tags. No socks. *No underwear.* Soft. He also (still) dressed in single colors or staunchly clung to cohesiveness. His plates, cups, forks, and spoons all had to be just right. A lot of this might sound like typical two year old's behavior, but his was more intense than anything I had seen prior and more so than I've seen since—until my current toddler who still is not quite there but close.

Stronger than typical attachment, epic meltdowns with transitions, particularity about objects and clothing, sensitivity to surroundings, obsessing about play and cleanliness, hypersensitivity to painful stimuli, and more, can indicate a struggle neurologically. Early intervention and parenting modification can significantly reduce difficulties later in life. Modifying our approaches to discipline can allow kids like this to feel like they have more control over their lives that seem to be spinning out of control. We do not need to give complete control, however. And in some cases, giving the illusion they have more control can completely shift their worlds. We know they don't really have all the control, but they feel like they do. From clothing choices to dishes and cutlery, we can let little things go. Flexibility in our parenting can help teach them flexibility too.

Decision-making is another piece of the *symptom* puzzle. Some are very impulsive and choose quickly. Others struggle to select anything, fearing that regardless of their choices, they will be wrong. And for fun, there are those who are a combination of these. Some choose and cannot adjust. Decision-making can be a struggle for many people, but for those who have neurodiversities like anxiety, options can be a crippling aspect of life. Once they have chosen something—a color, a shape, a pattern, a show, clothing—they cannot adjust. If change is forced on them, explosions and inability to function result. If given no time constraints or outside influences and input, people who struggle can come to a judgment. However, life doesn't happen in a vacuum. There are time pressures and limits. Often people who struggle try to adjust the world to meet their desires. Unfortunately, that doesn't always work. Inability to shift thinking resulting in complete shutdown is common in our house.

My son Will battles in his ability to make determinations. We were once in a store with a family member, Kait, despite my warnings Will was not okay. She had offered to buy each of the kids something. This shop was the last event in a full day. I knew Will was at the end of his patience. Kait was too. Will, as I anticipated, fought with himself over a choice between two toys he wanted. My husband, Leigh, and I took turns trying to help him. But his brain was sabotaging him. He was approaching disaster. Then Kait told us she was done and wasn't waiting anymore. Cue full-blown destruction. I took Will out of the store and sat with him while he expressed his emotions. Leigh handled the rest in the store. Kait and the others came out just as I had successfully reached Will's logical brain. The first thing Kait said was "If that's how you're going to act, I won't buy you anything!" Will started to break down again. I stood up and all but yelled for Kait to stop. "Greed isn't what this is about," I said angrily. Kait stormed off to the van. I held Will while he sobbed again. I told Leigh he'd better get Kait in line or I would!

I was thankful Leigh had chosen on our son's behalf and supported me against Kait. She doesn't understand. To her, Will was being manipulative and trying to get two toys. We knew he was struggling with deciding which toy he would get more use and time from. Which toy was worth the money? Which toy would last both from a fun and usefulness perspective?

We began to practice at home with Will and decisions. We gradually increased the number of choices presented and decreased the amount of time allotted. We also added distractions like music and light changes, which cause his brain to stumble more. We set timers and changed the scenarios. We helped him decide on a list of attributes he would like in a toy and how to mentally make pros and cons lists quickly. Now when presented with a choice between two desires, he is much more equipped. We spent months practicing. Though Will does better, he still needs more time and preparation than most.

The need to be perfect and right often comes along with this life. Perfectionism is also common but is more intense (seems like intensity is a heavy part) with people who struggle with anxiety. Again, precision is likely part of needing control. If they can attain flawlessness, they think they have achieved direction too. Subjective topics like decisions, art, and writing can be points of tension. Things with formulas and methods where there is no room for mistakes are preferred activities. Archery and martial arts are favorites in my house. We also do subjective things like music and art. Though we struggle, we must help them to learn how to handle and work through the frustrations of subjectivity.

We recently had an art project go awry because of perfectionism. Will was to draw a whale breeching the water and color his work per the instructor's specifications. The drawing alone had resulted in several explosions before Will and I were satisfied with his progress. He had accomplished most of the project and learned. So I declared the whale complete and explained to his instructor. Then we pushed through, and I had him do a simpler project so he could feel successful. We must help kids like Will strike a balance between defeat and success. Frustration is okay. Obstacles helps us learn. But too much causes paralysis. We cannot move forward or learn when we feel insecure. Following a meltdown with success is crucial for resetting the frontal cortex so we can move forward.

Sensory Component

For many children who are neurodivergent, there is a sensory component. They are either very sensitive and *everything* sets them off and they need to avoid feelings, sounds, tastes, textures, sights, etc. Or they need a lot of sensory input. I have one of each at least. And I am the former. I don't want to be touched. I hate incessant noise. Even people chewing can set off unpleasant feelings for me. Will is like me. He struggles with too much sensory input. Sights, lights, sounds, the feeling of clothes, shoes, and movement are a lot for him. He reads in the car, I think, to offset the feelings and sights involved. He also loves reading. Mack has big sensory needs. He touches or crashes into everything, hums, whistles, talks constantly, and craves the big, continuous noises and sights of life. Interestingly, he still doesn't care for certain types of clothing. He refuses socks, as do all my children largely. Underwear is a big no for both boys.

And as I write this, an annoying neighbor is playing loud, repetitive, mechanical-sounding music. My body is crawling. I have learned self-control though. These children feel this sense of overwhelm and cannot walk away or ask for it to stop. They are told they must deal with it. There is no solace. We can use headphones to drown it out, but they might hate the feeling. We can create a safe space and time where they can regain the feelings of normalcy and where their bodies don't feel edgy. But this method helps only after. We must meet them with empathy in the moments. Will asks for hugs when he is overwhelmed. When his brain and body are processing so much, I am his safe space. He can hug me and shut out the world for just a moment. He can breathe.

Mack has to learn the opposite. He must learn to express his needs in appropriate places and times. Climbing church walls and whistling during sermons are frowned upon. Jumping for a while before going to church and knowing he can stand on his head when we get home are good. He needs plenty of time to touch and tinker too. He is learning he may fulfill his needs at home, the farm, the park, the beach (he *loves* to roll in sand), and all sorts of other places. He is trying to learn touching all the walls at a mall or church is a problem because, while they feel good in the moment, the potential for a reaction from an allergen on the surface ten minutes ago is high. And that won't feel good. I have two opposite sets of needs to meet with my sons. And mine as well, though as with most things, I take a back seat. Will's general day is set up to avoid as much sensory input as possible. His room is as he needs and wants. He has intentionally organized his toys and books so they bring him peace. He practices martial arts too when he needs to calm himself. When we must be in crowds, I give him plenty of warning. He may also bring a book along so he may escape. Our friends' homes all have spaces where Will may go be in peace too. Mack's day, conversely, is arranged to give him as much sensory input as possible. The days we are at home, he can build with wood, do obstacle courses through the hall, and rub his feet on the carpet and dog. His room is managed so he has quick access to myriad of textures, colors, sounds. Mack takes movement breaks in between every school subject and may complete school in any setting he chooses. As long as his work is accomplished, he may hang off the couch to do so.

Notes

Chapter 2

Coping Strategies, Therapies, and Medications

Coping mechanisms are those things we use, sometimes without realizing, to help ourselves in tricky situations. For people struggling with anxiety, this is far more difficult than we might think. Remember people who struggle here are in their amygdales, the emotional center of the brain, during attacks and are thus unable to attain logic. They, and we as their caregivers, must find ways to recognize their triggers and their early signs of stress so we can help them navigate the enormity of their impending feelings. Eventually, they will be able to accomplish this with little to no outside assistance, but we must, with teachers, therapists, partners, and friends, teach them this skill. Each person will need a different tool, but through trial and error, their coping mechanisms can become an integral part of their day.

There are long-term survival tools as well as rescue ones. Meditation can help over time. People can learn to clear their minds of distress so they're not carrying their concerns into the next day or situation. They can also carry the skills into immediate situations. Breathing techniques are crucial for helping refocus. Contact with a familiar object or person can help achieve feelings of safety. A trusted loved one to hug or touch in times of heightened stress can be mood altering and grounding. Others might need to read or journal. Screaming about their stresses or *at* their apprehensions can be therapeutic. Drawing, painting, shredding paper, knitting, or crocheting can aid in calming the emotions. Workouts, such as running, cycling, martial arts, and climbing or gymnastics, might be another method to test for the fretful person in your life. Discussing activities the anxious person enjoys doing can help guide you to which coping tool to test first. Don't give up or change gears too quickly but listen to the person struggling about how they're feeling about each attempt. This is a difficult balance to strike.

Though martial arts, reading, and even drum playing are helpful to quell attacks in the moment for my son, they aren't always successful. I thought I was going to be able to pull him out of an episode by talking about his favorite subject: dinosaurs and paleontology. Dinosaurs worked once and I really thought I had figured out how to pull Will from anguish. The next attempt failed miserably, and rather than respond in giggles about my abhorrent dinosaur name mispronunciations, he screamed at me more intensely. Oops. I suppose I don't have this beat after all. Don't let these disappointments dissuade you from trying. They are just pieces of information to add to your arsenal.

Therapy can be a very helpful, but finding which therapy and which provider is right for you or the person you care for can be a challenge. Finding a provider who uses these can be as simple as an internet search. Finding one you work well with can be a different ball game so don't hesitate to "shop around" until you find the right fit. The right counselor can make all the difference.

Medications and diet can also be part of the plan, depending on the need and severity of the anxiety.

Play therapy is simple: you play. However, a therapist monitors the person while closely looking for certain patterns during structured play with a purpose. A parent or caregiver can also use play therapy at home. Toys can act out concerning situations in an overexaggerated manner with an extra dose of silliness to help ease the tension and stress regarding a particular struggle. Play therapy can be incredibly helpful for those for whom it works. However, this method isn't for everyone.

Alex was terrified of dogs. Breed and size didn't matter. They all elicited terror. At the suggestion and guidance of his therapist, Alex's mother, Marcia, decided to do some play therapy with Alex. Marcia set up some small dog toys along with various other animals that Alex was not concerned about. Marcia and Alex began playing with the toys. Alex gravitated toward the horses and giraffes and steered clear of the pesky dogs. Marcia played with the dogs and narrated a story about them running and playing. Alex, watching his mother, began to show interest in the dogs too. When he began playing with one of the dogs, Marcia chose a doll to play with the dogs. She animated the doll and the dogs running and playing together. She demonstrated the doll chastising the dog and the dog responding. Alex began to mimic his mother's play and got a doll of his own. Suddenly, dogs weren't so scary. He began asking to watch videos of dogs. The next neighborhood walk they took, Alex didn't flinch and run from the neighbor dogs behind fences. Several such play sessions and a gradual work up from small to large were necessary, but Alex became comfortable with dogs on leashes being within his eyesight. Later, he was even comfortable with touching a few trusted dogs. Play therapy worked for Alex.

Talk therapy is, too, simple. Talk. You find a comfortable, safe-feeling therapist who is trained in reflexive listening, and you talk. You may talk about your anxieties or events completely unrelated to them. Where the conversation goes is up to the person receiving the therapy. This can be therapeutic for some individuals due having control over the dialogue. The therapist opens a safe space and offers time and sensitive ear along with the occasional question or reflection. They may also attempt to target a specific difficulty the caregiver has described. The goal is typically to encourage the person with anxiety to realize their own triggers as well as what helps them come out of an attack or to feel safe and grounded after one.

Will engaged in talk therapy for about a year. During his time there, he was able to explore some triggers and feelings he had experienced but been unable to name. We often went home with manipulatives corresponding with a tracking method. One of Will's favorites was a red, yellow, and green light illustration. With the diagram, he could identify and mark how he was feeling. Green meant he was feeling happy and positive. Yellow meant he was between. Not quite upset or breaking down but not happy. Red meant he was in the danger zone. Explosion imminent. While we had discussed these feelings and their triggers before, the visual provided through talk therapy was helpful for Will's brain. Will attended talk therapy for a year before deciding he had gotten all the help he could from the counselor he saw.

Applied behavior analysis (ABA) is a common therapy in which the therapist seeks to alter a socially challenging behavior into one more commonly accepted. They use gentle techniques to teach how to operate differently when confronted with concerns. ABA uses a lot of practice about what to do in certain situations to retrain the brain to act automatically in the new (socially acceptable) way in real situations.

Cognitive behavior therapy (CBT) seeks to adjust the actual thoughts and feelings behind the actions. This is another targeted therapy in which gentle methods are used to retrain the brain.

Rather than changing actions, we're changing thoughts and feelings and generally eliminating them so the anxious person no longer feels the insurmountable emotions associated with the events.

In music therapy, individuals are taught to use music to calm themselves. They may listen to or create music. Regardless, music can change neuropathways in a positive way and assist in brain health and growth. Those who benefit from music treatment may also need another form of therapy to get the best results.

Jimmy has attended music lessons as therapy for two years. In that time, he has learned to meld into the music and allow it to wash over him. He has experienced release when he has pounded out random notes on the piano. He has achieved peace while rhythmically beating a drum. Jimmy has enjoyed the math of music as a way to make sense of his world. Whenever he feels anxious, Jimmy can listen to a song on his calming playlist or play a tune himself to regain composure.

Art therapy is another less conventional approach in which people can draw or paint. This can allow the seemingly undefeatable feelings to escape their bodies so they can recover and move toward solutions.

During her art therapy sessions, Judy has discovered a love for paint and chalk. The two mediums allow her to slam her feelings onto canvas in strikingly different ways. Paint over chalk is especially therapeutic to her because of the layering and texture produced. Her pieces are for her to keep and look at and critique or dispose of in whatever method she chooses. Judy likes burning them; the fire is cathartic.

Occupational therapy (OT) includes meaningful activities that can aid in helping people overcome obstacles in their daily lives. This can help them lead more peaceful and societally normal (typical) lives rather than ones fraught with constant fear. Gradual desensitization to objects or experiences causing difficulty are commonly included.

Kelly practiced wearing an article of clothing for a set number of minutes while engaging in other activities to become more comfortable with that piece. Her therapist increased the time she was to wear the article. And the distracting activity may decrease. Now Kelly can wear sweaters for an entire day regardless of what is happening around her.

Electroshock therapy is unfortunately still in existence today. Shocking the brain is an extremely controversial and painful way of attempting to alter brain connectivity to eliminate an undesirable aspect of a person. In short, a practitioner sends electrical impulses through the brain to change the transmission and reception of information. Though there is heavy debate, electroshock therapy is still recommended and used as a treatment in some cases. Here again, a trusted psychiatrist should be involved.

Alternative therapies, such as animal, dietary adjustments, and essential oils, saturate the market and make things confusing for parents and caregivers. Everyone swears a different therapy worked miracles for themselves or a child. The truth is sometimes they do. And sometimes they don't. If you feel comfortable with the information you're given and the research available and find a suitable center for your situation, there's probably no harm in trying one of these alternatives.

Equine therapy is one such type of alternative. In this method, an anxious person spends time around horses. They might do groundwork—leading, talking to, and observing the horse. They might ride too, thereby experiencing various kinds of riding and movements on the horse. Animal therapies of all kinds help a person become more in tune with their own bodies by being in tune with the animal. Animals teach us how to recognize feelings of concern and overwhelm in ourselves. One must watch an animal's body closely to discern feelings and safety.

Any animal can be therapeutic. Pigs, goats, cats, dogs, and donkeys can all be used in beneficial manners. In canine therapy, a dog may accompany a person to certain approved activities as the person's grounding and safety. Cows can be sources of comfort. Therapy cows will lie down and allow people to lie on and pet them. Simply running one's fingers through a cat's hair can help calm the mind and body. Pigs are social animals who will sit and engage in conversations with anyone who talks. Listening to a donkey bray helps ground people who are beginning to escalate. Looking into a goat's eyes while feeding grass also helps calm the body and regain logical thought. Animals can help those suffering from posttraumatic stress disorder (PTSD) learn to trust themselves and others again too.

Will benefits greatly from being at the therapeutic horseback riding farm where we volunteer. He has a routine that includes leading horses into the barn for breakfast and leading them back to their pastures. He has a favorite from each pasture whom he leads each day we're there. While they walk together, he talks to them or pets them. Will helps clean their stalls. The routine of leading, feeding, leading, and cleaning gives Will a sense of stability about his world. Feeding the cow, chickens, goats, pig, and donkeys is part of the routine too. Often Will will talk to the cow while she eats what he's given her. When farm happenings get chaotic, Will sits in the memorial garden overlooking his favorite horse's pasture. He talks to Teddy from there or goes into the pasture to get more cuddles. Teddy and Will have an understanding and often tell each other their secrets. We have seen impeccable changes in Will since beginning work at the farm more than two years ago.

In the laundry list of what different people will tell you about "fixing" anxiety, autism, ADHD, ADD, and so on will be dietary concerns. They will likely include red dyes, gluten, dairy, processed sugars, carbs, folic acid for the MTHFR crowd, and probably more items you should avoid with your child. They will probably mention supplements your child *should* take and foods they *should* eat. This is a challenging list to wade through and make sense of. Working with a trusted practitioner—whether your PCP, neurologist, psychologist, psychiatrist, or someone else—a professional's input is encouraged. Your child may very well struggle more when gluten-rich foods are in their diet. Or not. Red dye, or any dye, and sugars may cause significant problems, even in small amounts. Or not. Those who have children diagnosed with MTHFR (a genetic mutation affecting the body's ability to process and store synthetic folate known as folic acid) know folic acid can increase symptoms of neurological and other disorders. Avoiding the processed folic acid and switching to methylfolate tends to help these people function better. My son fares better when his daily meals are spread not more than three hours apart and include protein and fiber along with fruit or vegetable. We learned his blood sugar stability affects his ability to moderate his explosions and recognize his feelings early enough.

We learned about Will's need to eat a balanced meal more often when a friend suggested he might be hypoglycemic. I don't know why I hadn't considered this before given I am also. After checking with our primary care physician (PCP), we started feeding Will as though he struggled with the same issue, and within a week, he was regulating better. We even noticed moments of heightened dysregulation when his schedule for meals was disrupted.

As overwhelming as the life of a neurodivergent parent or caregiver is, different diets may help with regulation and behaviors. If you're going to change a child's diet, a physician must monitor progress. Changing a diet can result in a child not getting enough of the essential nutrients needed for brain and body development, so a medical practitioner, such as a dietician, input is important for this. The dietary changes should be continued for several months consecutively and strictly so change can occur. Often a detox period initially further upsets a child, but after some adjustment time, we can begin to track changes. After several months of strict adherence, if there is not noticeable change, another diet can be attempted. A rest period between each is appropriate too. Changing diets too quickly or cheating during diet attempts can upset the whole process and deliver questionable results. This is not an easy or simple task to accomplish, but the right diet could make a significant difference in your child's ability to regulate emotions and responses if an appropriate dietary method is found.

In severe cases, medication may be required. A psychiatrist will need to determine and prescribe any medication. However, other therapies are likely necessary along with medication. Continuity of care is also vital as the changes brought on by hormones in and out of puberty can significantly change the severity and reactions from anxiety. Medications should also be closely monitored as they can have an effect contrary to the desired. If a psychiatrist recommends medication, they will first order blood tests to determine safety and efficacy of the drugs chosen. The psychiatrist will also closely follow your child to determine whether the medication is correct. Diligence in reporting any positive or negative effects will be critical to the success of any treatment plan. Failure to utilize a licensed psychiatrist can result in addiction and misuse of medicine.

While therapy is a necessary path, medication may need to work in tandem. A psychiatrist can prescribe and monitor medications while a psychologist can facilitate therapy. The following are some of the many options for medications and their basic uses:

1. Antidepressants, as the name suggests, are stimulants. Some work by increasing serotonin. This is a neurotransmitter affecting mood, sleep, sexual desire, appetite, and memory. These kinds of medicines tend to take time to build up enough to help with anxiety, but the wait can be

worthwhile. The side effects are rather mild and include nausea, dizziness, dry mouth, muscle weakness, drowsiness, and sexual dysfunction. If any of this is a significant issue for you, a doctor can help with alternatives.
2. Benzodiazepines are sedatives that help relax your muscles and calm your brain. They increase certain neurotransmitters, which are chemicals that relay messages across the brain. By increasing these specific transmitters, more of the right messages get through. They are usually used short term as they can cause habits and difficulties with balance and memory. Careful monitoring is needed because of the side effects of depression, dizziness, headaches, and confusion. Weaning off them suddenly can cause strokes too, so careful down dosing is required.
3. Tricyclics are also sometimes used, though not as often. They work similarly to the above but with more side effects. They are rarely prescribed now.
4. MAOIs or monoamine oxidase inhibitors are also used less frequently due to their more severe side effects. They were approved initially to treat depression but also work with anxiety. There are also restrictions with MAOIs, such as not being able to eat cheese or drink red wine. Certain medications also interact with MAOIs in a dangerous way. Communication with a doctor is crucial if using one of these drugs.
5. Beta-blockers, often used to treat heart conditions, can also be used for anxiety. Particularly in stressful situations. While they don't usually cause side effects, some possibilities are fatigue, dizziness, drowsiness, dry mouth, trouble sleeping, nausea, and shortness of breath. If any of these is a significant struggle, your doctor should know.

Sometimes a psychiatrist or psychologist will offer alternatives to medication in the form of home remedies. Cannabis, exercise, and essential oils can be effective in gentle treatment of milder anxiety.

As with any illness, communication with a physician is a top priority. Self-medicating at home might be a great option for you, but many medications for treating anxiety have interactions with other medications and even with herbs and oils. If your physician isn't working with you on a treatment plan, you may need to find a new practitioner. There should be a trust and communication between doctor and patient so the patient can find healing or stability.

This is a wonderful resource for more information on different anxiety medications[1]

---

[1] https://www.drugs.com/condition/anxiety.html?category_id=&include_rx=true&include_otc=true&show_off_label=true&submitted=true.

Notes

Chapter 3

❃

Progress and Regression

Progress is when we see massive improvement after months (or years) of struggle. Colossal improvement as the result of hard work, hours of therapy, and probably tears. This is a time for rejoicing. We can actually breathe, finally. We are tempted to ignore this and feel we don't deserve this time of reprieve and rejoicing. Ignore that feeling. Rejoice. *Please* rejoice. This is crucial. We cannot continue to work if we don't stop and rejoice in the good times. Even a little reward is good. Take it. Relax. Breathe. Enjoy.

Will struggles with changes in routine. I left up a daily schedule we had followed when I was regularly babysitting a toddler named J. I needed to rotate whom I was working with on school while J remained entertained. Then we stopped watching J. I didn't change the schedule though. Will still wanted to adhere to his school break times we had used for his times to play with J. But she wasn't there. After a few weeks of him asking for the time because it was his time, he finally told me he was just following the schedule. I recognized this as a win because he was telling me the issue. We worked together to write a new schedule and work in times for him to rest.

Progress can also come in the form of a caregiver fitting in a missing piece of the puzzle. Leigh fit another piece of Will's puzzle recently. We have dealt with a lot of grief with Will with the losses of horses in the last two years. Leigh suggested Will might be using his grief as a crutch to not have to address current struggles. He was struggling with his brother Mack, and we couldn't get to the bottom of the issue. We asked Will to mediate and think about the struggles. He ended up thinking of his horse friends who've died. We weren't able to get to the true route of the specific issues of play the boys experienced, but we did figure out this important puzzle piece. Will does tend to call sadness over the horses as an out to addressing problems. Now that we know this part, we can work with his therapist to help him avoid avoidance. We can also be aware, as can he, this is a crutch he needs to work around and not rely on.

Unfortunately, on the flip side of progress is regression. This is particularly frustrating as we know we have worked hard to reach a goal and suddenly progress vanishes. We see and enjoy the light. But the victory becomes a loss before we fully grasp the win. This is, perhaps, the most disheartening part about parenting these children. We feel like we are going back to the very beginning.

We recently experienced a time of regression in our house. Will had been doing well with food. He was trying new things. He was branching out. He was willing to eat things that weren't his favorites. Then he wasn't. He might have eaten bacon last week, but not anymore. He might have tried cabbage and powered through a month ago, but not tonight. I felt like he was punching me in the gut. I felt like maybe I was doing something differently with cooking because he was no longer enjoying foods he'd eaten well the previous week or month. Leigh and other kids were fine with the foods. This should have told me he was the issue. Not me. But as we all are, I was my own worst critic. I knew my son's difficulty with food again had to be my fault somehow. Leigh repeatedly reassured me it wasn't. Maybe I almost kind of believe him.

After my own meltdown, I took some deep breaths and remembered Will's struggles with food were in no way a reflection on my cooking or work to provide his body with what he needed to thrive. I remembered our methods of relaxing regarding food. "Try it. If you don't like it, make a sandwich. If you like some, eat what you do like."

This hasn't been our only regression. He has also struggled more with compromise, crowds, unmet or adjusted expectations, changing routines, and more. This is not my fault. There is nothing I can do to change the regression. I have to just be there and encourage him to take his time to process. He had a lot of big expectations placed on him at summer camp at our beloved farm. He loves being there. But when the routine changes and there are so many more people, he struggles. This week, he is a helper when I need him. Next week, he is a camper. This week, he is struggling. I do not know how next week will look. We have a lot of conversations about how to react to the different schedules and people. It helps *some*.

If I give Will as much of a plan for the day as possible, I can set him up for success. I can go over with him each change I can anticipate potentially occurring. We can plan how he might react. None of the potentialities may come to fruition, but at least we are both prepared for the potential. At the farm and at home, Will knows he has safe spaces to escape and breathe. Providing these spaces for decompression and allowing the time needed to clear their heads can be monumental for people who struggle as Will does.

Regression is part of life. As new parts of the brain develop, others take a back seat. As big tasks force a part of the brain to be more heavily activated, other parts rest so they can take up the slack later. These patterns eb and flow throughout the formative years and into adulthood when our bodies and brains need to focus on some other more complicated tasks. There are certain periods when our brains are developing at a more rapid rate, and these regressions in other areas will be more apparent.

Sleep

There are many conflicting resources regarding sleep. Some sources say the developing brain needs more sleep. Others say gifted brains need less sleep. Some parents say their kids thrive on little to no sleep then complain, in the next breath, their kids act up all the time and cannot regulate. Again, each situation is drastically different. However, we know scientific method research shows sleep allows restoration to the body. Sleep allows the brain growth to occur from learning all day. Sleep allows memories to form. Without sleep, science says we die. Sleep is as important as food for brains.

So what do we do with those kids who seem to be able to cruise through life without sleep as though they're Energizer bunnies? This question begs a look into what exactly about sleep allows the restoration, memory formation, and brain development. There are a few theories about what parts of sleep allow these things to occur. We need them all. This site (https://www.verywellhealth.com/why-d o-we-sleep-the-theories-and-purpose-of-sleeping-3014828?_ga= 2.119566600.1253137745.1548117366-1566229980.1548117354) suggests sleep flushes our systems of the hormones that cause us to feel tired in the day and of neurotransmitters that were used to make meaning but are no longer needed, thus making room for new ones in the new day. Very Wealth[2] purports that the above functions, and more, are largely accomplished during REM sleep. REM is "rapid eye movement," and it is a period of very deep sleep when the body restores and rebuilds itself from the day. There are several stages of sleep too. And each is important for a different reason. As outlined here[3], REM and NREM (non-REM) stages of sleep are both important and helpful. In part of the NREM stage, growth hormone is released in children. The consequences of inadequate sleep here are obvious: impaired growth. In REM sleep, the eyes move quickly and indicate vivid dreaming. Scientists also believe REM to be crucial to making meaning and memories.

So when people are not allowed appropriate sleep, some of these things can fail or be compromised. Some people need fewer overall minutes of each of the stages, but every stage is equally important. There are, however, eighty or more known sleep disorders. Each of them can cause disruption to any of the above processes, which are crucial for growth and development. Identifying and treating sleep disorders is not simple, however. Recognizing there may be a sleep problem and seeking care are important to lifelong health. Sleep affects the brain, but it also affects the body. Poor sleep in infants and toddlers can lead to obesity in young children and into adulthood. Having parents with poor sleep habits or with sleep disorders can also be a predictor for children to suffer similarly.

While many think gifted people need less sleep, this study determined additional, more specific studies were necessary. While many parents of gifted individuals report sleep disturbances, the

---

[2] https://www.verywellhealth.com/why-do-we-sleep-the-theories-and-purpose-of-sleeping-3014828?_ga=2.119566600.1253137745.1548117366-1566229980.1548117354

[3] https://www.verywellhealth.com/the-four-stages-of-sleep-2795920?_ga=2.144407221.1253137745.1548117366-1566229980.1548117354

study does not support this as a giftedness issue. There are many factors that play into sleep difficulties. Giftedness may be one, but it is not the only, and it has not been proven. So if your child does have difficulty with sleep disturbing his or her daytime abilities to learn and regulate, a visit with a sleep doctor may be necessary. Whether your child's giftedness is the cause of the sleep troubles or not, a physician's involvement and support are necessary.

Along with a physician and therapist, we can create environments at home that lend themselves to better respite. Eliminating screens with blue light for an hour or more before bed helps the brain adjust to the outside darkness. A calming routine with gentle music and reading assists in the body relaxing for sleep. A foot or back massage lulls children into a restful state. Lavender essential oil and melatonin are options too. Tart cherry juice even supports the brain's transition to sleep.

Brain development

Our brains are complex and confusing. We know little about how they work or how to predict how we will grow and develop. Our surroundings have a lot to do with brain development and personality, but much of it is also nature. Rory, Will, Mack, and Kae have all been raised in very similar environments. They have all had the same genetic pairing for parents. They have all had much the same parenting. We differentiate a bit because they are different people. While they have all had similar childhoods, they are all very different from each other. And even as different as they are, they have all experienced similarly timed but different kinds of hasty progression. Their brains or bodies have experienced rapid growth that has left us reeling from the whirlwind of major brain development.

Several expert psychologists studied brain development and

discovered a few static courses people tend to follow through childhood. Jean Piaget[4] studied the developmental arc of children and asserted that younger children are not dumber than those older but simply process and think differently. As they age, these processes evolve and become more sophisticated. During the sensorimotor stage, infants develop motor skills and object permanence (that even when they cannot see an object, it still exists). As they complete the needs of that stage, they move to the preoperational stage wherein they develop language, memory, and imaginative play. Following preoperational toddlerhood, they enter the concrete operational stage. In concrete operational, they begin to manipulate information with symbols related to concrete thoughts. They also begin to lose the egocentric nature that was present during preoperational. The final stage is formal operational. During formal operational, people begin to apply abstract thought to symbols. Most don't complete the final stage until adulthood.

You can see that an infant who should be only developing basic thought can struggle because they understand the world in a way they cannot physically access or demonstrate. A very young child may be able to imagine big things but becomes frustrated at not being able to discuss them. The ability to think and process beyond language abilities can also lead to some fears or even anxiety. Children who can manipulate symbols and abstract thought but lack the emotional maturity or life skills to apply them can become frustrated as well.

Maslow also has a theory about how children develop. His refers to emotional (highgatecounselling.org.uk/members/certificate/CT2%20Paper%201.pdf) well-being and maturation.

According to Maslow, we must have lower order needs met

---

[4] https://intranet.newriver.edu/images/stories/library/Stennett_Psychology_Articles/Piagets%20Theory%20of%20Cognitive%20Development.pdf

before we can progress to more sophisticated ones. Our physiological needs, such as food, water, shelter, and warmth, must be met first. If any of them is lacking, we cannot progress to the next level of safety. Safety includes physical and mental safety along with stability and freedom from fear. After those are accomplished, we can begin to think about belonging or love. This is when we are able to accomplish meaningful relationships with others within a family, friend group, or significant other. We then are able to ascend to the self-esteem level. We can achieve mastery and respect here. Finally, self-actualization is the step during which we can pursue an inner talent and feel fulfillment. Unlike Piaget's developmental stages, these are met depending on accomplishing the previous level. The ages are not static here. Like Piaget's theory, precocious children might attempt to scale them all at once and become frustrated. There is nothing we can do to stem this frustration or attempt at greatness aside from ensure steps one through three of Maslow's hierarchy are solidly met. The final two stages are personal and internal. And though most don't meet the final stage of self-actualization until well into adulthood, many of our precocious children seem to achieve it sooner.

The first two years of life carry the biggest change in brain function a child will experience. These first two years are rampant with language development, physical development, understanding of the surrounding world, learning who they are, learning who we are, and emotional development. Children are confused and questioning through age two at least. They have a lot going on. They need tons of reassurance and connection. Our job, as parents, is to provide encouragement.

Two was when Rory decided she knew more than us. She knew the appropriate way to dress. When it was acceptable to play outside. Will wasn't yet very verbal, but he certainly knew what he wanted. He knew those cars and dinosaurs needed to be lined up just the right way. Mack was wild. He climbed everything. He figured out how to open our three-step baby gate to the kitchen. But he knew what foods would hurt him too. Kae decided diapers were no longer acceptable. She yearned to be read to and demanded many books each day. She also knew she would play violin.

Age three is big too. They start to really assert their independence. They figure out they have brains separate from ours, and they are learning how to use them. Figuring this out takes trial and error. They are in a constant state of "What happens when …?" They don't know how to ask theoretical questions but are masters at experimentation. We need to let them explore. But we need to set firm boundaries to their exploration. We need to be consistent most of all. If the rule is we all stay at the table until dinner is over, then we do. It will become normal. The boundary won't be tested any more. They know where the limit is. If we keep moving the boundary, we confuse them. This applies to more than kids at age three. We must be consistent always. Lack of consistency means uncertainty to these little brains learning what the big, scary world is all about.

Kae has tested our will regarding holding boundaries. She is almost four now but doesn't quite believe us when we say how life needs to work. She still doesn't believe us when we say the dog will nip her when she is rough with her, yet she gets nipped every time. She knows she can do heavy lifting and clean stalls like the big kids. She can't. She tries anyway. We are beyond exhausted with admonishing her at this point. She demands repeatedly for all things her little heart desires. She rarely takes no for an answer without a tantrum. We have yet to give in to one of her tirades, but she tries multiple times each day anyway.

The next leap in our house tends to be around age six. They might be able to sit longer periods and focus on bigger tasks. But those bits of progress didn't come without trial. So much more whining here. Struggles when things didn't go just their way. I found my children forgot how to perform simple tasks when their brains were tackling huge new concepts. The hormone changes and regulatory systems seem to clash and cause a kind of storm. Mack, who couldn't yet read when age six hit, could soon after. But he forgot how to put away his clean clothes. Perseverance when they are leaping is pivotal to surviving the growth. I couldn't let Mack out of his clothing responsibility because he was experiencing brain growth. I just had to remind him multiple times each week about what laundry day actually means.

Nine has been another big one for us. The hormones really start changing around age nine. Their brains are doing big things with figuring out sexuality and impending puberty. Their bodies are also changing drastically. They're beginning to put away *childish* things like dolls and action figures in favor of more grown-up things like technology (where allowed). Rather than play pretend with her friends or siblings, my daughter started wanting to listen to music and create art around this age. My son has spent more time alone and reading or practicing drums. Of course, how these leaps are executed will differ greatly from child to child and house to house, but the basis of it is things are changing and we need to be prepared to meet them with love and compassion.

The night before Will turned nine, I told him it was his last night as an eight year old. He had a breakdown. He didn't want to turn nine. He didn't want to grow up. When we recently cleaned out the playroom, Will also reacted poorly because he didn't want to grow up and holding onto the toys he's played with for years was a way to maintain the childhood. My disdain for clutter makes it difficult for me to be gentle in this situation. But lots of hugs and reminders that his well-loved toys can bring joy to others helped him part with many. We still have more to purge, but this is a start. I learned years ago I can only ask for little bits at a time.

In my research and crowd sourcing, I have seen ages twelve and fifteen tend to be rather large leaps too. At twelve, puberty is really beginning to rear its ugly head for a lot of our young people. Their hormones begin raging. Girls begin menstruation, which can be very scary. Boys begin having erections at random times and wet dreams. These are scary times for their changing bodies. Even when the most well-educated children begin puberty, they can react strangely. This may come out as defiance or sassiness. It might be a lack of motivation or caring. Regardless of how it manifests, puberty is scary. It is a huge time of change, and we need to be well prepared for it.

Rory is entering adolescence now. She is getting hair in places she didn't before. She is beginning to stink. Her hair is getting greasy more quickly. She has to shower more often. She hates showers. She knows her menstrual cycle is impending and most of her friends have already welcomed theirs. Rory has also entered a lovely stage of knowing better than anyone else and picking fights with her siblings. It seems like she feels she has something to prove. Will and Mack often complain about her tone of voice. She tries to assert herself as an authority when she isn't, and her siblings react poorly to it.

Rory is now experiencing a sort of coming of age period. She isn't comfortable in her body or brain right now. She doesn't want to be known for being intelligent but doesn't know who she is outside that. She told me she felt like a trophy. I held back tears as I waited and listened to her rail on how I talk about her to others and how much she hates it. I took deep breaths as I asked her how she wanted me to talk about her. Or whether she just doesn't want me to at all. I told her I would deflect questions and let her shine for herself as she wants. She doesn't know who she is or who she wants to be, but I know I have to get out of her way and let her wings spread in whatever direction she needs.

Other parents tell me children around fifteen or sixteen start to find their parents unintelligent. I am certain we have all experienced the superiority of our children prior to this, but the know-it-alls ramp up during the teen years. Teens look at their parents as though they were born yesterday and the teen is the one with all the life experience. This reaction is due to the forthcoming need to spread their wings and strike out on their own. Burgeoning independence slightly earlier makes this transition easier. Not that the transition into one's own life as a young adult is easy on the parents but perhaps just a bit easier if the teen is expressing more individuality earlier on. I think open honesty is key in these years. If we are honest with our kids and create a safe space for them to be honest with us, we are more likely able to correct the potential missteps of precocious teens. But these teen years are not when the open communication must start. If not well proven early on, open communication patterns will be difficult if not impossible to cultivate with established teens.

While your home may not follow this progression, we must realize there are periods of rapid brain and body growth along with hormonal changes affecting the way our children perceive and interact with us and the world. During these stages, we need to remain consistent but also adjust to what our growing children need. We cannot treat our budding tween as we do our stubborn teenager. They will resent being spoken to and disciplined as such. However, if we are consistent with our young children, we stand a better chance with our older ones. Furthermore, if we do not look at parenting as a war we wage against our children but as a journey we walk together, we stand a far better chance of maintaining relationship with teen and grown children. Even precocious, twice exceptional ones.

As I begin to embark on the journey of raising a teen whom I have raised from the beginning, I see how my relationship with her as a young child influences our relationship now. She is more open with me than her friends are with their parents. She still feels safe crying to me and telling me her dreams and goals. She is only twelve, but I am hopeful her openness will continue.

Notes

Chapter 4

❀

Discipline Methods

Discipline looks different for every child. Everyone has a different personality and one-size-fits-all approaches are ridiculous. Sure, there are some great theories out there on child-rearing, but when it comes to the nitty-gritty, sometimes they just don't work. And our kids seem to have read the books and decided to scoff in the face of every method purported as the end-all to parenting. Don't misunderstand me. Those methods and those books that have failed me are working for others. There is, typically, nothing wrong with them in general, but they're not right for us. You're reading this because they're not right for you either.

Discipline means to teach or guide. So often we think it means something big and authoritarian. But discipline is teaching. Teaching involves explaining, listening, showing/modeling, and correcting. Some children are simpler (not easy—simpler!) to teach/discipline than others. Some children happily follow instructions given by their authority figures. I know if you're reading this book, your children do not. I also know you are as desperate as I was (and am) to find effective discipline. I do not, by any means, have teaching right or perfect and my kids still step out of line, but the methods we have tried (and failed at) and those we have stuck with might help you.

As any new parents, we talked to our babies from the minute they were born. We read to them, sang to them, held, and rocked them. I nursed them (constantly) and held them while they cried. In desperation one day, I laid my firstborn, Rory, on the floor because she'd been crying so much. I needed to step away. To my astonishment, she stopped crying. This child didn't want to be touched anymore. She was my infant who nursed all the time, but she was telling me, even at two weeks old, she needed her space too. I am glad I listened to her. Here, discipline started. She had told me something, I had listened. My goal at the time wasn't to make her stop crying; babies cry. That's okay. I needed a break. My break resulted in her stopping and being happy instead of touched out.

We continued discipline by telling Rory we needed to change her diaper or bathe her and though unpleasant, it was necessary. She'd squirm and cry and we would talk or sing her through and acknowledge her feelings. As Rory got older and got teeth, we had to teach her not to bite. Then mobility meant teaching her certain things were unsafe for her. Repetition didn't matter to her. I have always heard consistency is key in these pretoddler times, but she didn't respond to no and moving away. She'd go back. All day long, for weeks on end, we would move this child and she would go back. She finally stopped when we told her why something wasn't for her. "No, that will hurt you." Rory's eyes and body understood, and she stopped. From then on, she almost asked with everything before touching.

As a toddler, she knew what she wanted and knew how to get it. She abruptly refused to wear the clothes I had chosen for her one day, insisting she didn't want to wear those and she could dress herself. From that day on, until about eight, she dressed herself. Around eight, Rory began a shift in clothing needs and suddenly required assistance again.

Rory is twelve now and still logical. Give her a reason (which she finds sound) and she will happily go along. She is a bit better about arguing her position and capability now than she was at nine months old but, we rarely must put our foot down about anything with her. She expresses frustration at times about our well-reasoned answers that she even agrees with, *but* she doesn't stray. She really doesn't need much parenting in this stage of her life. We're friends. She talks to us about everything (for now), and she trusts us. We trust her. We will see how things change in the next few years!

Our next child was a fairly easygoing baby. Will was slower to smile or laugh. He was thoughtful. He was emotional. Discipline with him used to be pretty simple too. He didn't really try much that wasn't going to be okay. The bigger issue was when we needed to change activities or go somewhere new or leave a place he wasn't prepared to leave. Even preverbal, Will told us he wasn't ready, often by screaming and throwing his chunky baby body to the ground. Walking away from the screaming as is often suggested did *nothing* to make the ear-piercing screams cease or make him follow. We had to wait. He wasn't crying for attention. He was in fight or flight. Even at age two. Changing gears was threatening to him. Transition still is, but at ten, he handles it slightly better *sometimes*. At the time, we thought Will was displaying extreme toddlerness. He wasn't. Now we know Will was struggling with anxiety. When we gave him *lots* of warning and transition time, he fared better, though not always and not perfectly.

He would also melt down when his toys, about which he was very serious, were accosted. That's how he thought of any disruption, I'm sure. Will's meltdowns were the only place we really had to assert any discipline in his earlier years—before his brother came along. We tried *everything* to get him to stop screaming. We spanked him (not proud of it, but we were desperate and realized quickly this was *not* the right answer; a swat didn't work anyway). We tried telling him to go scream in his room and be happy in the family area. We tried taking toys. Nothing. Nothing worked. We needed to change our perspective. He is a feeler. We had to accept his feelings and let him have them as long as he needed to. Then he could come to us.

Will wasn't verbal until around age four, so him telling us what was going on wasn't possible until then. We would just hold him until he was ready to get down. We reassured him we loved him, and he was perfectly welcome to have his feelings. He never really wanted hugs *during* a meltdown but after. So we were and are there. Every time. His breakdowns used to last for several hours, but as he's gotten older, he often comes to us and talks to us about his battles before they reach disaster status.

We also know Will is very stubborn. (He *might* get that from his mother.) He knows what he wants or needs and when. When those things aren't met on his schedule, he can become explosive. Blue is his favorite color. I don't care what color utensils they use. He does. If, for a reason he doesn't accept, his spoon is not blue, he will lose composure. People say to choose your battles. This is a battle I don't choose. I make sure he has the blue spoon. No one else cares. However, when they have a question of who does which job or leads which horse at the barn and other people *do* care, compromise is necessary. We are working on improvement. Sometimes Will does okay and he is able to compromise. Other times, he's not and he melts down and misses out; work doesn't stop because he stops. Sometimes he's able to take an alternative.

For instance, when I ask him to empty the dishwasher while he is reading a book and he didn't know ahead of time he was next in the rotation. Often he will ask if he may reach a stopping point in his book and then whether he may listen to music while he works. These are typically things we can agree to. However, if the dishwasher is clean, there are dishes all over, and I need to prepare a meal, he might not be able to do things in his desired order. In this case, I will explain to him the difficulty with his suggestion, hug him, and let him know I will be in the kitchen with him and he may read after he finishes his job. This doesn't always work either and he ends up screaming in his room before coming to do the dishes. If so, I prepare the meal on the table (if possible) or move dishes to the table so I have stove and counter space, then when he's ready, he accomplishes his responsibility. But by now, the others have eaten (I won't hold their food) and are playing while he must work, then eat, then do as he pleases. He's missed out on the reading portion because he was unable to get the closure he wanted.

Refusing closure seems cruel, and as though I could just allow him to read as he asked initially, but this doesn't help him gain flexibility or understand others depend on him to get their tasks accomplished. And as always, after the ordeal, we are sure to hug on him as long as he wants and talk through why this time was a challenge for him. Often there is some other event he'd been attached to and thinking about and the dish need was too much. He wasn't really ever being manipulative or belligerent. He was struggling.

We have had to change our language to fit how his brain processes information. That is okay. Everyone is different and our job as his parents is to create a safe space for him to grow and learn how to make sense of the society he is part of. He is an incredible, smart, loving, stubborn (tenaciousness is a good thing, trust me) little boy who is going to change the lives of everyone he gets to be around.

Our third child is another boy: Mack. From the beginning, he was a challenge. He was born with over sixty food allergies—some life-threatening and others not. He was unsettled and itchy constantly. He threw up daily. He was covered in eczema, which is a painful, itchy rash. He'd scratch until he bled. I had to avoid all his allergens to heal his gut and his skin. He didn't sleep. Ever. For his whole first year.

Despite health struggles, he was on the go. He rolled at three weeks and crawled at five months. He pulled up in a hospital crib fewer than twelve hours after general anesthesia at six months. At two, he had sedation for a CAT scan but didn't sedate. Mack is now eight and still hasn't stopped with the physical gifts. He learned to ride a bike without training wheels on the second try. He tore up a wood deck, board by board, by hand with his friend. They were five and six. Not only is he on the go all the time, but I couldn't let him out of my sight. He was going to figure out how to escape from the house, climb the roof, and attempt to fly off. Or worse, pick up the infant we babysat and walk around with her like a rag doll. Or he might bite someone. We had to teach Mack to growl and make fists when he was upset, which was our cue to remove him so he could calm down and talk. Prior to teaching him this skill, he was aggressive. He routinely cornered his older brother and sister and beat on them. Whether he was just entertaining himself or gaining control as the youngest child with significant restrictions, we don't know. We do know he needed to be watched so he wouldn't truly hurt anyone.

Until Mack was around three, he was always in eye shot *or* I took the baby with me. We let him go a bit around three because he had shown he could follow directions for a little while and be fairly reasonable. However, I often had to return to a discipline method called "tomato-staking." In this method, the child never leaves the caregiver's side. Regardless. As a tomato plant grows up best with a stake to hold straight, so a child like Mack fairs quite well with constant supervision and reminders. Yes, I was exhausted, but the result is lovely. I now have an eight year old who is permitted to go outside alone. Unless his deck friend is with him Those two cannot be trusted. He can do his own laundry and put away dishes. He can even watch his three-year-old sister for short periods of time in relatively controlled environments. Sure, he forgets what "put away" means from time to time, but when reminded, he usually does so without a fight. He is *always* ready to smile and laugh and do tricks like backward flips off the couch and standing on a horse. He is sweet and thoughtful too—when necessary.

When he doesn't clean his room after searching for a desired toy, he is not being rude to me or his roommate. Mack's mind is on a toy and the game associated. He isn't thinking about putting back the containers his toys live in. When reminded to do so, he (almost always) does so without complaint. Usually with a sigh and an eyeroll because he *knows* and forgets. Often I must go and check his "clean" room as I know it really isn't. I will point out what he's neglected to put away and help him neaten up if needed.

We used to watch Mack fold and put his laundry away because he would fold one item then get distracted. Again, struggling with remembering something rather than intentionally ignoring a household rule. Even I did that at the farm recently. I forgot two cardinal rules and had to be reminded. To which I responded, "Yup, I know. Thanks for the reminder." Then I shook my head as I walked away because *yeah, I do* know, and I forgot. When he is overly forgetful or being hurtful in some way, I will stake him again. Just for a day or so to remind him of where his brain ought to be.

The same methods of digging for a reason for Mack's struggles are not as effective on this child as they are on my older son. Though they aren't as effective, finding or recognizing the root of an issue is still important. We just struggle to find the cause. Mack's age might contribute, but I think he is just wired differently. He isn't typically thinking through things very far or for terribly long after they occur where his older brother, Will, carefully considers before, during, and after so he's more able to access those pieces and motivation. We are just obligated to address difficulties as they come with this one, but future plans don't tend to work well. With maturity and modeling, he is becoming much more thoughtful and we notice, acknowledge, and thank him for his increased thoughtfulness.

My last child, Kae is three. Most people think the "terrible twos" are the worst part of toddlerhood, but really, three is worse. Kids think they know things at three. Of course, my kids have tended to hit the next stage a bit earlier so we're almost out of three. The year of "Why?" and "Myself," and "No, I do it."

Like with the others, we started disciplining Kae at birth. Remember discipline means we're teaching them. She would pull her hair during diaper changes, so we covered her head; holding a newborn's hands while changing her diaper is impossible. We were helping her learn not to pull her hair. We told her why. She loved bath but not the cold part after. She hates clothes but is learning they're a necessary part of polite society. However, we allow nakedness at home. She has learned how to use the toilet instead of a diaper, but she regressed so we helped her remember by gently reminding her to go try. Sometimes she protests. Other times she goes willingly. Sometimes we miss the window and have an accident. Sometimes she piddles and stops and tells us she needs to go. Sometimes the same happens with bowel movements. It's okay. She's trying and improving.

She *must* put on her own shoes. And clothes. Generally backward. She doesn't always agree to us fixing them. We do (or not) through her protests. "I'm sorry you don't like this, but your shoes won't fit this way. May I show you a different [better implies her way is wrong or bad] way?" She protests, and I proceed then offer a hug. Sometimes she fights and throws herself. We pause, calm down first, and then proceed. She doesn't accept no as an answer very well. She asks why and we tell her, only for her to ask again.

She runs away from us when we ask her to come—sometimes. Sometimes we just have to let her scream at us through what needs to happen then hug her while she calms down. Or she screams for a while after being told no about something and we offer her hugs, which she sometimes accepts, or she may sit on the step and scream then come when she is ready. We find allowing them to entirely control how and where they express themselves (as much as possible) is helpful in their ability to regulate and move on. We don't need to decide when they are finished feeling. We need to be available when they need us at the end.

Discipline is tricky. Teaching isn't one size fits all or even most. We have four biological children whom we've had to teach in very different ways. We have thus far had five exchange students who were teens we have had to approach differently. We have a new one now, and she needs something completely new. That is okay. They are individuals. Life would be boring if they were the same. We have breached dating, sex, internet use, porn, cell phone use, clothing, marriage, communication, and more with our teenagers too. Those are struggles I believe we set the foundation for success in when they're toddlers and preschoolers. Our teens are going to be much more willing to come to us if we react in love and support and a heart of discipline rather than in judgment and harsh tones now.

I don't know how Rory will evolve, but I am sure we will have more anxiety—different anxiety—with Will, and we may tomato-stake Mack again too. Kae is a wild card at this point. Regardless, keeping the teaching in discipline will serve us and them throughout our parenting time. Discipline—teaching.

At the root of our discipline model, regardless of the child we're directing, is a simple belief: children who aren't acting as we desire them to are rarely doing so to upset us but because they're struggling. Sometimes children truly don't want to do what we ask of them, but often, there is some underlying struggle they're experiencing prohibiting them from compliance. Finding the root of the difficulty is paramount to moving beyond it. Sometimes you can reach a compromise.

Parenting experts like Alfie Kohn encourage giving kids power in as many situations as we can. Let them choose the plate color. Let them choose what to wear and how to keep their rooms. The outcome of giving kids power is supposed to be more cooperation. Our kids laugh in the face of our attempts to placate them and convince them to do things.

At two, Rory told me she didn't approve of what I had chosen for her to wear. "Fine," I said, "dress yourself." From that day on, she did. Until she didn't anymore when she was eight. Then she wanted help again. Mack and Will never really cared about their clothes. Except to care the clothes were soft, lacked tags, seams, and buttons, and didn't itch or otherwise cause discomfort. Kae has been the biggest clothing struggle. If she had her way, she would wear fancy dresses to work at the farm in the mud, then be perturbed she dirtied them. I cannot convince this child of anything. I only hope her stubbornness will serve her well later in life.

No amount of explanation or logic will win them over. Only force. And we hate to force things. Soon they will acknowledge the importance of toothbrushing in preventing cavities and will acquiesce to the task painlessly—or at least, we hope they do. Thankfully, as they get older, we can sometimes reason with them a bit better and they can tell us what the issue is, so we can address the root of the problem. Force is still needed in some situations but becomes more difficult to use because they get bigger. Desensitizing therapy through ABA or occupational therapy (OT) is helpful when we need to accomplish a task they resist.

Along with finding the root of the problem is finding the right way to communicate with each child. Not only about the root but also about the behavior. We often try to address different people in similar ways, which doesn't work. Everyone processes differently, and we must choose our words and tones to reflect variations. Sometimes finding the right fit for diverse people is challenging, but when we do, both parties experience great relief.

I know what tones and words to use with each of my kids *for now* because I am always with them. Sometimes Leigh struggles because he isn't in the everyday, though he's very perceptive and involved. I might not always address every kid as is best for that child because I am not with them constantly. Observing and listening to them and watching their responses is paramount. More important is, if possible, watching the people who are with them all the time or asking a parent or primary caregiver for input. As an adult, I can ask for more information or for a different tone, but a child might not feel comfortable doing so or may not realize it is necessary. Our job as adults is to suss out and apply the needed method, so everyone can communicate and work through issues cooperatively. When we make mistakes here, we must recognize and rectify them. Adjusting attitudes and relationship building are important to continue productively. Sometimes an apology is needed as well.

I was babysitting one of my nephews and he kept arguing with everyone. No one could say anything right. I chastised him firmly and a bit too harshly. I had already battled more arguments than I could count between him and Kae and I was over the fighting. I interrupted him and shot him down. "Stop arguing and get outside now, or sit on the couch and do nothing." He immediately complied, but I later learned arguments are an expression of anxiety for him. I could have addressed him more gently. I could have paused and taken the time to listen to him about his concerns and address those rather than abruptly ending it and *winning* my way.

Even when I do know the right tone to use with a child, I don't always use it. When I am overly frustrated, I struggle too. Just like them, I make mistakes. Kae does not listen well. She is learning, but it is going slowly. Ruby, the dog, told Kae to back off. She didn't. Ruby reacted. Kae got nipped. The nip hurt but didn't break skin. I screamed at Kae and crated Ruby firmly. I don't want Ruby to resort to biting, but she needs to protect herself. Kae needs to listen and now that she's received what we have predicted, maybe she will. After screaming at Kae, I relaxed and apologized. She's not permitted in the same room with Ruby without Leigh or me. He and I can keep them both safe and teach them appropriate interaction. The others, try as they might, aren't firm enough with either Ruby or Kae.

Word choice. Tone. These are crucial in communicating. They are more important when dealing with those who struggle with anxiety. When addressing a person who creates scenarios without their input or control, choosing the wrong words or a harsh tone can spell disaster. They are more likely to decide something is going to go wrong if your words are carefully specific. If your tone seems irritated or off in any way, the anxious person will struggle.

Often when people hear us being choosy with our words and tones with Will they think we're being too soft on him. Too permissive. In reality, we're appealing to his logical brain and helping him through something that would prove challenging and result in a meltdown if otherwise addressed. Similarly, when we address a meltdown gently, we are seen as pushovers. On the outside, we seem to give in to his screams, but we're remaining calm so he knows he's safe to express how and what he needs. Hugs while he's screaming are uncommon as he doesn't want to be touched. But big cuddles once he has resolved are necessary. He must reconnect and feel safe again so he can talk about his feelings. He melts down because he's trying to run from a threat. People assume he is screaming to get his way rather than because he fears losing something. He tries to keep control of life in a manageable way to him. To others, it looks like he wants to control every aspect of every day. He's expected to just let go and follow the way others are rolling rather than being met halfway. His brain simply cannot just let go.

After a busy week of farm chores with unforeseen extras, we decided the family needed a day off. A day to reconnect and chill together or separately. The lack of routine and expectations was a problem for Will. He needs to know what is going on. Not to control it, just to know. His brain works better that way. Leigh gave Will a rough rundown of what the day would look like so Will could calm his brain and enjoy the downtime. A simple task of giving expectations likely prevented meltdowns.

Will needs some semblance of predictability and control so his brain is free to play and learn. Pressure to perform or do something new causes him to freeze entirely. These requests must be handled lightly and with a great deal of support and patience.

We didn't learn about our children's discipline and communication needs quickly or easily. We had to use trial and error. We also employed a method of questioning Dr. Greene describes as collaborative problem-solving. In his book *The Explosive Child*, Dr. Greene lays out a method of deep questioning geared toward specific issues our children may be facing. The goal is to elicit from the child the root of the problem. Once the child has identified the source of their own struggling, the parent and child work together toward a solution. The objective is to come to a method that leads to success for both parties. A recent conversation with Will went as follows:

> Me: Will, you seem to be struggling today. What's up?
>
> Will: I don't know.
>
> Me: Can we work through some ideas?

Will: Sure.

Me: I noticed you had trouble with your math. Were you frustrated about it?

Will: No, it was easy.

Me: Good. How did you feel about your practice time?

Will: It was okay.

Me: Just okay?

Will: Well, yeah. It wasn't perfect, but I am working on it. That's not the problem.

Me: You struggled with talking to your brother about a game to play. Was that it?

Will: No.

Me: Can you think of other things?

Will: Well, our schedule has changed so much, I think I am just not sure what to expect.

Me: Okay. That makes sense. You do struggle more when things are less predictable. What do you think can help you?

Will: Can you make a new schedule for the wall? That way I can check it and know what is next each day?

Me: Of course. I would love to.

Not every conversation goes this well. Mack seriously fights this type of questioning. He always answers that he doesn't know. He isn't as self-aware as Will yet. I hope he will get there and we can find the sources of his difficulties too so we can work toward solutions that work for us both. For now, all I can do is work against the immediate challenges. I always feel like I am micromanaging him.

Those unwilling to meet children where they are, regardless of their diagnoses, are quite unfit to be involved with those children. We cannot expect children to learn and feel safe when they're being told who they are is wrong. When children's brains are working to achieve monumental tasks, they often struggle with everyday needs. We need to give their brains a break while they conquer their worlds.

Several people have studied motivators and discipline to determine the best methods to use across the board. We know that no two children will respond the same way to the same disciplinary course, but we can understand the motivation process so we can better access the choices that will help our children best. Abraham <u>Herzberg,</u> BF Skinner, and Edward <u>Thorndike</u> are three such scientists. They studied motivation, rewards, and punishments.

We know now children and adults are more likely to succeed in areas they enjoy regardless of environment. And if we want them to succeed in other areas, we may need to adjust the environment to suit the learner better. I see from my own children that they are more than willing to complete school tasks they enjoy but have to be cajoled into the rest. Often interspersing topics of interest with others helps them succeed.

We also know people adjust their behavior when outside influencers are present as with rewards and punishments. Often parents let nature help by allowing natural consequences to occur. For instance, I may have warned my child that climbing the chair may cause him to fall and get hurt. When my child continually fails to listen to my warnings, I might allow him to fall from the chair, enduring minimal injury and temporary pain. The child will have learned a valuable lesson and will, hopefully, make wiser choices in the future.

Notes

Chapter 5

Routines

Routines can be helpful for children who need predictability in their lives like those with anxiety or autism. Also, those who are just more comfortable knowing what is next. However, routines can and do change. We need to help our children develop some flexibility. Often the assistance comes down to the words we use to indicate change. With some children, we can simply say plan A isn't happening and leave it there. Sometimes a plan B suggestion is necessary. Sometimes we must present plans A, B, C, and even D or more and the contingencies that would cause each to occur. Furthermore, sometimes we need to present it in a way the child thinks they are making the decision rather than someone else thrusting it upon them.

Static events like dinner, bedtime, and some other predictable routines are necessary to anchor the child to something familiar, so those changes are slightly less scary. Preparing them for change can also be helpful. Including them in the decisions to change are too. When we talk to Will about changes, we must tread carefully. Letting him know we need to chat and he might struggle is important. Next, we let him know a new plan is forthcoming and explain thoroughly why we can't accomplish the initial plan. For instance, we'd planned on going to a museum with his grandparents when they were visiting, but in choosing the trip, we realized the museum was closed on the day we'd intended. Immediately, Leigh went to see if he was awake still so we could tell him and he had time to adjust and process. He handled this time well, but the minute he got up in the morning, he asked what we were doing. He asked over and over until we had a decent answer. He did well this time. Other times, he's cried and needed hugs and time to process the change. Still other times, he has screamed and taken a long time to adjust to the idea of change and still not fully recovered. He's better, and lots of warning and recognition of his need to process and know the next thing help significantly.

Some people who struggle with anxiety, autism, or other neurological disorders can't adjust to changes. And when there are less than desirable behaviors, we want to change the plan to meet them where they are. The funny thing is sometimes they are already in the plan in their minds, but we are not there with them mentally or physically. We work with a young man, Q, who has had the routine changed because of behaviors he exhibits while anticipating the scheduled event. Anticipation releases hormones like adrenaline that can increase unpleasant feelings. Q's aide is very in tune with him and has encouraged the school to continue with his schedule amid these challenging behaviors. We see great change for the better when he comes to do what he clearly loves. We and the aide report this positive step and continually encourage the school to extend his time at the farm with us and to make a more permanent, regular schedule for him to be there. When we have people who calm and regulate during certain activities, we need to ensure the consistency of those activities. For this young man, the horse farm is a place of regulation. The strategy can remain unless unsafe to do so. In this case, behaviors do not make the plan unsafe.

For some, we can reason and employ logic and help them understand change. Stimming and meltdowns due to change are common. Having a contingency to replace a missed opportunity is crucial to success. A comforting activity like meditating or calming colors or textures can aid in regaining logic. A room or corner with the materials they need or want to help them achieve balance is helpful. Will has a relaxing jar he can shake and watch the glitter settle. Q enjoys doing puzzles to calm his body and mind. Mack likes to build. This is a safe space where they can regain the control they feel they've lost.

Food

Food can be a huge stumbling block for neurodivergent kids. Parents want their kids to eat healthy diets. Our kids tend to be rather unhelpful in this arena. As all humans, they have preferences, likes, and dislikes regarding food. We offer a large variety of colorful, healthy foods and they end up subsisting on apples and carrots. Dream scenario, right? They eat a fruit *and* a vegetable. This is better than cheese sandwiches or chicken nuggets exclusively. Food can be a battleground. We are never sure what way to wage the war either. If we go in too hard, we meet a lot of resistance and the standoff is ugly. If we go in too soft, they win immediately. Food is necessary to survival. And we need them to eat *something*. This battle day in and day out is exhausting, so we give in. *Just eat.* We plead. They do. But it isn't necessarily good.

In our house, we try hard to not wage war in this arena. From early on in starting solid foods, we set clear expectations and mealtimes. We eat often. They are able to make choices about the type of food and preparation. Junk foods like chips and cookies are not available. Ever. They just aren't in the house. The rules are simple: eat something from each food group before repeating. This ensures a balanced day. Dinners include a protein, a vegetable, and sometimes a grain. These things are served upon request and in small portions to ensure success. We encourage tasting at least once. A simple substitute may be made for the vegetable or protein. Repeat of the favorite is not permitted until the other offerings have also been tried. Breakfast, lunch, and snacks are entirely their choices within the parameters of ensuring each food group is represented throughout those four mealtimes. I keep a treasure trove of fresh fruits and vegetables in the house. I keep healthy fats and proteins like almonds, sunflower seeds, almond butter, and hummus for vegetable dipping. Plain yogurt with real maple syrup added also serves as a dipping sauce for fruits and vegetables.

This plan evolved over many years of strife in our house. I had initially adopted a method friends used. They saved what their kids didn't eat at the meal for the next time. If the kids didn't finish dinner, their leftovers were breakfast. They were not permitted other foods until the previously uneaten had been finished. When Will didn't eat for more than twenty-four hours using this plan, we knew we needed to change something. This wasn't stubborn. This was bigger. We gradually made it to the method we now use. We have a lot more pleasant meals.

These may sound like lofty goals and a lovely house without food fights. There are absolutely food fights. There are times I work really hard on a meal to be told it isn't appreciated. I am often tempted to *actually* let them starve—for a meal. I am tempted to stop arduously meal planning for weeks in advance. Carefully planned meals to suit the vegetarian and the food allergic kid and the particular one—and the husband can go. I am tempted to just quit and see if they notice. But I am not heartless. I know they struggle. I take a deep breath, count to ten, and refocus. Or I walk away and Leigh deals with dinner. We work through. Usually after I yell. I am purposeful about purchasing fruit and vegetables I know they eat regularly. I am purposeful about planning meals they love. When I am going to try something new, I ask for them to taste it. I have low expectations. I stopped telling them what was in dishes so they would taste without preconceived notions about how it would be. They can mostly figure it out now. I am considering blindfolds for new foods.

We don't want food to be a battleground. We know food fights can lead to eating disorders of all kinds. We don't want to lie about what is in foods. So we tell them after they taste first. I settled for one fruit and one vegetable for Will. If he tries something else, I rejoice. I know kids who won't eat anything called fruit. So the parents don't use the term. And I know parents who use peer pressure to encourage trying new things. "Johnny is eating olives. Why don't you taste one?" Maybe they magically stumble on a new like. I know of people who put a variety of foods in a muffin tray set within the kids' reach. When the tray is completely empty, Mom or Dad refills it. This also encourages autonomy with food. Kids are choosing what they eat, how much, and when. But a well-rounded nutritional base is still available.

There are some extreme cases. Kids who really and truly won't eat anything except tried and true staples. Parents have tried every suggestion and are at their wit's end. The kid needs food to live. We feed what the kid will eat. However, we don't give up. We try feeding therapy. We use smoothies (if they accept them). We use meal-replacement shakes to get the necessary nutrients into their bodies. Vitamins too. But we don't stop trying to get a larger variety. We rejoice with every victory. And cry with every setback. We rejoice when we find families struggling with the same thing too. You see, there is power in commiserating. There is renewal of strength in finding togetherness. Hearing success stories also renews our strength.

Food can be a battle. We don't have to allow it to be. We can realize our children struggle—with taste, texture, newness. We can come together with them and help them learn to love life-sustaining foods. Food doesn't have be oppositional.

Notes

Chapter 6

Parenting Together

The arrangement of the parental unit differs in several ways for various children. Regardless of the situation, there is generally some need for cooperative parenting of children. This gets sticky. When we are dealing with delicate children and must, somehow, be in agreement with another human also dealing the delicate children, life gets complicated. The beauty of the world is we are all different. But that gets tough when we have to make decisions about someone else. Our ideas and opinions differ. Our execution differs. We must learn to listen with love to what our partner is saying and feeling. Counseling may be needed for coparents to get on board with one another. Family counseling might also be necessary. We are proud of choosing therapy rather than embarrassed. This choice indicates we desire success and to display respect through working together.

Disagreements on how to handle situations, discipline, school, family, and more will arise no matter how close and respectful the parents are. Neurodivergent children challenge us to our core. They make us reevaluate how we do life and love. The reflexive listening I outline for siblings can be helpful here. I learned this skill with Leigh while we were in premarital counseling as a technique for couples to use to really understand one another. Remember this technique is about listening to each other for understanding rather than responding. The practice forces us to truly listen rather than prepare our next statement. This system will lead to better compromise and understanding. I also like to pause, think, and ask follow-up questions of people so I *know* I understand. I will even respond to them using what other meaning could potentially be interpreted so they have an opportunity to be understood.

Ken and Jerry have not learned reflexive listening yet. Their conversation follows.

> Jerry: Ken! This house is disgusting. You're just home all day. Why isn't it clean? I am starving. Where is dinner?
>
> Ken: Whatever, Jerry. The kids were terrible. No one helped with anything. I haven't made dinner because they've been at me all day. I can't even breathe.
>
> Jerry: I don't care. I work hard all day, and the least you can do is the same.
>
> Ken: Make your own dinner. I'm going to bed. You deal with the kids. They didn't stop barking at me all day. I couldn't even get dressed without someone else needing something!
>
> Jerry: Don't you walk away from me! You need to clean this house and make dinner!

Ken: Do it yourself.

Ken and Jerry clearly struggle to hear each other and respond calmly. The following is the result of years of practice and many deep breaths. Bob and Janet have learned they are working together in life and need to communicate effectively to accomplish their goals. They have deep respect for each other and the daily struggles each experiences.

> Bob: Janet, I am really frustrated the house is a disaster when I come home from work!
>
> Janet: Bob, I hear you saying the mess frustrates you. Why is that?
>
> Bob: Janet, I don't know! Maybe because work is stressful and I just want calm when I get home. This mess doesn't give me a calm feeling.
>
> Janet: I hear you saying the mess overwhelms you when you get home. I want you to look forward to coming home.
>
> Bob: I do feel overwhelmed!
>
> Janet: I struggle to keep the house tidy though because of the kids, cooking five meals each day, and my own needs.
>
> Bob: I hear you expressing time sneaks up on you at the end of the day and you feel a lot of pressure in a lot of places.

Janet: Yes! I feel like you understand! How can we meet both our needs?

Bob: What if you set an alarm for an hour before I come home, and you and the kids can go through and tidy up. You shouldn't be doing it yourself. Half of it is their mess.

Janet: Okay. I think we can. I do like my alarms. Can you be more understanding when the house isn't tidy when you get home? Most of the time, we can probably have it neat, but there might be times we can't.

Bob: Sure. I think I can.

Of course, this won't solve every problem. We know stress plays a part in parenting struggles. And special needs children are among the top reasons for divorce or separation. Arguing and unrealistic expectations are listed in the surveys, but both of those struggles are common with parenting in special circumstances. Seeking outside assistance is imperative when parents are struggling to come to common ground with their different children. The vast disparity in opinion is crippling. Expert help is required to address the differences.

A new person assimilating into a family with a special needs child may experience significant difficulty with the transition. The new person might be familiar with the struggles, therapies, medications, and diagnoses involved but doesn't make jumping into the middle easier. Kids with autism spectrum disorder (ASD) or anxiety often reject new people entirely. If the child does accept the new person, he or she may struggle to accept the new person as an authority. The roles of mom and dad are engrained in the thoughts, feelings, and behaviors of these children. Attempting to step into a parental role is daunting. Even impossible. And assuming parental duties might be contrary to those previously enacted—even more so. Furthermore, depending on the age of the child and the reason for a new relationship (the reasons of which may not be apparent), the child may feel the previous parent is being replaced. Children require reassurance the new stepparent isn't replacing the previous parent. In some instances, the child can be involved in what role this new parent might fill, which can be helpful to the transition. Family counseling is crucial when changing the family dynamic so drastically too.

The struggles associated with shared parenting are common regardless of the children. But the arguments become more frequent and troubling when there are medical or mental diagnoses to discuss and plan for. The expectation of a "normal, healthy child" is trampled and we have to reconcile what we're gifted. The amazing, precious, precocious humans with multiple big, complicated needs really throw us initially and even throw seasoned parents off their path. Navigating struggles with the person you were initially parenting with is its own challenge. Changing the paradigm and family roles further complicates familial relationships. Respectful communication is key to being successful at parenting together.

We cannot be afraid to communicate with each other. I asked Leigh to help me with the kids' music practice woes, knowing he was working in the daytime and evening is dinner and bedtime. We don't have time for them to practice at those times. I know he started to say he couldn't possibly ensure they were practicing. But he changed his tune and said he would do what he could. He then shored up my explanation of what practice should look like routinely. I know I sound like a broken record to my children and when someone else affirms my words, they are more likely to listen. Had I not asked for his help, he wouldn't have known about the struggle.

Parenting Struggles and Support

Parenting is a hard and lonely job regardless of the kids we have. We no longer enjoy the village lifestyle wherein large groups of families lived together or near each other and everyone cared for all the children cooperatively. We are almost entirely alone. Unless, by some stroke of magic, we stumble upon a friend or two with whom we can share the journey. Your parenting partner is integral, but nothing compares to a good friend with whom you relate on a different level. Finding support is especially important when parenting neurodiverse children. Someone who won't judge you or scold you when you rant about your terrible day that made you want to run away. The kids were over the top and you're exhausted and need someone with a loving ear to cry to about feeling like a failure. There was a therapy setback and you already strategized with the psychologist or psychiatrist and with your husband, but that is not enough. Friends are important. Taking time for yourself and not feeling guilty is crucial to successfully parenting challenging children.

Friends are also crucial for children. Someone to walk through life with. To laugh with. To cry with. Parents can be incredible helpers to their children. Siblings too. But we're just not enough. Kids need others near their age with whom they can let loose. There are no expectations. Just fun. But when we think about our kids, we don't see others who are like them. They're the outliers. The ones who don't fit in. We must be creative.

They have to work harder. Approaching someone and asking them to play isn't simple. At least not for these kids. They must know something about someone else first. They need to know they're not going to be completely rejected. They observe. They gather information. Then they make calculated movements to increase their odds for success. When they succeed, balloons are almost necessary to celebrate.

Of course, not all neurodiverse kids are this way but many are. My son Mack could make friends with a wall. Will and Rory aren't. Sure, they're friendly enough, but they're deep and need someone to match. Mack is charismatic and sincerely doesn't care what others think, so when he needs to talk with someone, he just does. Making friends is easy for him. The others, we have to help.

In our current age of technology connecting people from nearly every socioeconomic group, country, race, culture, and generation, relationship is difficult. We may feel we have accomplished rapport for a fleeting moment, but they're not who they said they were. We sign up to meet people or do group activities and we're underwhelmed with the selection. We meet people who we think "get it," but we listen to them talk and maybe they do a bit but not in the way we need. Or their struggle is completely different. These real-life connections are difficult for us as adults and parents. They're nearly impossible for our learning, developing, insecure children who really don't fit in and don't understand why. We try to help them. Our attempts are often misguided. They're noble. And sometimes, they result in incredible relationships for both parents and children.

Rory and Will have expressed frustration in being unable to find their fit with friends. I was easily and quickly able to find the perfect match for Rory. I know this sounds like a sleazy matchmaking web site deal. I crowd-sourced in online groups for children like her and we met in a public place. I was shocked at how well the two girls got along. One tall (not my daughter) and already ten. Long, flowing, blonde hair, and so sweet and soft-spoken. The other, short, nine, short, bobbed hair, sweet but not so soft-spoken. That is my daughter Rory. But the two of them were instant best friends, bonding over their love for Harry Potter, precious stones, art, and jewelry making. Now they're planning on playing a duet together and they talk daily. I enjoy the mom and sisters too.

So when Will expressed a similar need, I went straight to my groups. I described him. I initially got nothing at all. Several months passed and he reminded me, so I tried again. This time, *lots* of response. Half of the four families we have met seem (at the moment) to be decent fits with our lives, beliefs, and personalities. Will likes both too. A big perk of both is there are siblings of similar ages to my other children and those of our younger friends. The other half were not so great. They just didn't mesh well with our lives. Unfortunately, though we tried to continue connecting, the friendships never flourished. We have not been able to help him find his fit yet. We won't give up.

We need these extensions, these friends. But we don't need "friends." True friends are similar with some differences but who can, through those differences, teach us something and us them. Glaring differences in fundamental aspects of life choices just spell impending disaster. We must recognize the difference between uplifting and crushing. Particularly when we're helping guide our vulnerable children through this tricky friend making process. They'll appreciate us steering them away from a potentially harmful situation, but we shouldn't help every time. We need to allow them to learn this skill of detecting good friends too. And unfortunately, we need to let them hurt about friendship lost. Furthermore, we need to encourage them to keep company with unlikely people. Their friends, our friends, don't need to fit in neat little boxes of the same types of people. Diversity is important. Friendships with those you share a few things in common but with whom there are a few differences. We even need to encourage friendships with people who have a different moral code. Or who might not speak kindly. Our kids can be positive influences and helpmates to others. Just as others can be to our kids.

We model what good friendships look like to our children. Our own friendships serve as guides to them. If we keep company with those who use rather than support us, we are modeling a dangerous relationship. If we associate with those who judge us and are always asking for change, we are demonstrating a dangerous friendship. When we maintain friendships with those who compliment, help, and truly love us, we prepare our children for healthy, lasting friendships.

I have three such friends in my life now. I had good friends in high school and college, but life happens and they fell away. Some couldn't handle the food allergy restrictions. Others chose very different lives and we just didn't fit anymore. Four years ago, two women fell into my life through the same mutual acquaintance. They didn't know each other, but by spending time with them separately, I knew they would be great friends with each other too. Last year, another woman, whom I met because of a moms' group, became part of our tribe as well.

We are all very different. Saucy has three children who are nine, five, and four. Mack and Sawyer are great friends. They are the two who tore up my deck together. Beth has two adopted children who are three and five. Rory has acted as mother's helper for Beth on several occasions. Dani has four children who are twin six year olds, three, and one. I babysit for all four, or some combination, regularly. Saucy and Dani work and their kids are in daycare or school. Beth stays home with her three year old while her five year old goes to school. I stay home and take my kids to work with me. Dani and I are more religious. Beth and Saucy are not. Dani is recently divorced and navigating the sharing of custody and new people pieces of life. I have been mostly happily married for thirteen years. Leigh and I are partners in life. Beth and Saucy are also married to good men who share in the caring of their children, but they went through lots of life to get there.

We have similarities and differences. We love each fiercely. We share each other's successes and sorrows. We share parenting and marriage woes. We drink wine and coffee together while laughing over the silliness of our children who are all neurodivergent in some way. Our husbands offer to care for the children so the wives can be together alone. We have family holidays together. We share in birthdays, births, and deaths. We are family more than friends.

My goal with my friendships is not just support for myself. I hope my children learn what friends do for each other. I want them to see friends make allergy safe thanksgiving dinners to include everyone. I want them to see friends drop everything to throw wet things out of a flooded basement. I want them to see friends rallying together with one who is sick just to be there for them.

Parental Struggles

Parents and caregivers of children with mental differences often begin to struggle themselves. The self-doubt can lead to anxiety and depression in the adult too. The friend and family support systems are integral to the well-being of the entire family. But therapy may be necessary for the caregivers and/or siblings. Support therapy sessions for the whole family together or individual members can help everyone understand each other better and encourage more open communication.

Recognizing a parent or caregiver struggle while caring for a neurodivergent child can be difficult. We are often preoccupied with what is required for caring for our children that we aren't paying attention to ourselves. We need others in our corner to help us see those times, but we need to be gentle with ourselves too in processing the information we need to provide proper care for others.

Sometimes we struggle as parents with things unrelated to our children. We're people too. When Leigh started changing yet another set of brakes on the van, he was not pleased. Several weeks ago, he replaced the front set. Then he changed the brakes on his car. Then the rear brakes on the van. Not only that, but he also got sick this week and was weak. He had to pause on the brakes and do the other side later. In trying to get the tire off, he pulled off a lug nut cap because the mechanic had overtorqued the nut. Then he broke a breaker bar (long ratchet) trying to get the nut off. We called our roadside assistance place and a mechanical socket wrench did the job. But he couldn't then get the piston back where it needed to be. So we called a friend of a friend. Before they got there, he finally got things where they needed to be.

The week was stressful for him. None of these stressors came from the kids. I had a stressful week too because I was trying to pick up what he couldn't do. And Mack was struggling with control, so I have had him attached to me almost constantly. We are exhausted. And stressed.

Leigh plays video games for stress relief, which doesn't always work. He just needs time and space. I must remember. I need to write, read, or gorge myself on junk food and wine while watching my stories. Whatever you need to do to release the immense stress of parenting neurodiverse children, do. Encourage your partner to do theirs as well. If you haven't found your niche yet for stress relief, you will. Take up a hobby, learn an instrument, invent something. But feed yourself. You will not be able to sustain the marathon if you don't take a break.

Parental Rivalry

A game parents tend to play by pitting their unsuspecting progeny against one another like they're miniature fighters hoping to somehow come out on top. "Mine slept through the night at two days old." "Mine was a pro at nursing—never had an issue." As they age, we get more complicated with tasks like walking, talking, reading, sports acuity, and more. Everything is a contest. Henry runs fastest. Jane reads more books. Penelope is the best soccer player. Jake is the best artist. We want our kids to succeed and do well and—dare I say?—be better than others. This is not part of the friendship I share with Beth, Saucy, and Dani. We compare bratty things our kids have done instead. We build each other and the kids up. The fourteen kids we have between us know we all love them and celebrate with them daily.

We need to, for the sake of our impressionable children who must live with these choices, shift our paradigm. We need to celebrate each of their strengths, shore up their weaknesses, and teach them to do the same for others. We aren't all the same, nor were we meant to be. Joey may be incredible at life sciences and terrible at math, but that's okay because Lola is a natural with numbers and entirely disinterested in life sciences. Teaching our kids to celebrate differences is crucial. They will be much better humans if they can learn this skill. Not only can they help others with their self-esteem, but they can help themselves too. They can ask others for help in areas they know they struggle with.

We try to provide opportunities for them to work collaboratively so they can see each other shine. We help them praise one another on jobs well done. We showcase their strengths rather than their weaknesses. Leigh and I demonstrate our strengths too and help each other with weaknesses. We don't shy away from showing our kids our weaknesses either. We let them see us discuss struggles and come to solutions together. Sometimes ours chats are kind and follow the reflexive listening pattern well. Other times, we struggle though we've been practicing the method for years. Regardless of the ease of the interaction, we always come to an agreement about how to proceed with our children. Or one of us compromises and agrees to try the other's method for a time.

    I encourage my boys to do this daily. Mack is skilled at figuring out engineering and building concepts while Will is better with fine manipulations and reading. They can help each other if they will only admit they need one another. When they can come to the realization they're not lesser because someone else does a different task well, they can move mountains together. When they can polish one another's crowns and realize their own aren't tarnishing from the task, they can overcome any obstacle in front of them. But therein lies the rub. They can't often arrive there. The place where they can be humble enough to acknowledge the other is better at this concept. They think they need to be good at everything and when they struggle, dissent is much worse because they shouldn't struggle. Everything should be easy.

    I used to think Rory would slow down in academics when they got more challenging. She didn't until college level work this year. Physical tasks like riding her bike are hard, and she has no interest in continuing because she stops having fun when life gets hard. She is stubborn. I reminded her when she finally decides to set her mind to a task, she can conquer anything quickly. She needs to decide she can and then she does. The struggle is a state of mind. Rory texted me she would need an accompanist for the piece she is arranging herself for recital. Two minutes later, she texted she didn't. She just needed to work hard and fast. My heart swelled. We just had tears about violin struggles and inability to overcome difficult pieces. I just reminded her she can when she decides to, and her decisions make all the difference. She decided. She overcame.

Will shuts down when tasks are too challenging. He has to step back and work up to the more challenging aspect again another time. He conquers. He overcomes like Rory. But he has to step back and take a mental break from it before being able to revisit and win. When we recognized his needed process, we were better able to facilitate him. I know he needs to sit in quiet and work through his thoughts. I build that time into his day. Realizing what our children need and providing space for them to be themselves is critical.

Notes

Chapter 7

❦

Immediate Family Involvement

When there is a special needs diagnosis of any kind, the whole family is affected. Siblings, parents, grandparents, cousins, and more can be directly affected, depending on the family unit. Many parents of special needs firstborns choose not to have more children while others choose to add to their families. When families grow, siblings must learn to cope and understand the special needs family life. This can be challenging for neurotypical children and also for otherwise gifted family members. Teaching everyone coping skills and communication skills is crucial to familial happiness and success. Teaching these skills at home in isolation can be challenging. Many families seek assistance through counseling and occupational therapy. Often siblings and parents or one or the other attend counseling along with the special needs child. They can all learn better how to communicate and coexist through this mediation.

Reflexive listening is a coping skill often taught to couples seeking marriage but is a skill all of us ought to employ. Listening to listen is the base of this method. In this active form of communication, the listener considers what he or she has heard and repeats it back to the speaker in his or her own words.

I mediated a conversation regarding toys recently in which I reminded my children how to do this. The conversation began rocky because they all wanted to be heard, but they needed to listen first.

> Will: I don't like the tent you guys built because it is too big and in my way. I don't like how I feel going under and it's too dark to see what I need. I feel like the poles are going to break too. You didn't make it right.
>
> Me: Will, let's be careful with accusations. Let's talk just about your feelings. Rory, do you understand Will's concern? Can you repeat it in your own words?
>
> Rory: Yeah. He doesn't like the tent I made for Kae because it is in his way.
>
> Me: Will, is that right? Do you have anything to add?
>
> Will: Mostly. It's just that I am afraid the poles will break from how you built it, Rory.
>
> Me: Rory, how do you feel about it?
>
> Rory: I don't think there is an issue with the poles. I was careful. I only built it because when you made us take the last one down, Kae had that fit about wanting a tent in there. So I built her one because you asked me to.

Me: Yes, and I appreciate you helping your little sister. Perhaps we can come up with a compromise on another, smaller tent that isn't in the way of other toys but still appeases Kae. Right now, you need to just put away this one because I need to make dinner.

Will: I think we need to rearrange the playroom to make the tent Kae wants.

Rory: Oh great.

Me: We can explore that, but I will need a plan from you about what you think will work. Rory, relax. Just take down this tent and we will continue working on solutions.

Rory: Okay.

Kae: No, my tent!

Me: Kae, we will make another one, but it will need to be out of the way of the other furniture and toys.

Kae: Okay, I guess.

Mack: Why am I here? I didn't care about any of this. I didn't build that tent. Do I have to take it down?

Me: I need to make dinner. Mack is my helper tonight. The rest of you go put away the tent.

In this exhausting conversation, I taught them again how to listen to each other and work together toward a compromise. I almost had to cajole Kae again because apparently she really loves having a tent over her desk. She was surprisingly amicable to the temporary pause on her desires.

Many siblings feel left out or less important because of the time and energy parents and others spend focusing on the special needs child. Ensuring time for neurotypical siblings is crucial to avoid these feelings. Each person in the family has independent value and must be treated as such. This can be very taxing, especially in larger families. Ensuring each child gets the individual attention they need takes time and money. Time and money tend to be scarce for special needs families too. Extravagance is unnecessary. Quality time can be spent with a child doing something simple like visiting a library or park. Ensuring each child has something special to share with each parent is the important part. Parents also have to be sure that the time, though not equal, is equitable. Quality time is more important than the quantity of time.

A date to the library with one parent. A trip to a favorite store to look at silly toys and send pictures to grandparents for Christmas or birthday gift ideas. Some time in the shed with a saw and a 2x4. Simple. Free. Time spent together.

Raising one child with special needs is a demanding position. Any addition increases the demand. Parents often bear the weight of these burdens alone which can lead to marital problems as well. Parents seeking therapy to ensure they are communicating well and meeting the needs of their own relationship rather than only that of the special needs child(ren) is also important. Not only is communication crucial, but so is time with each other. Time with each child is important, but parents cannot neglect their relationships with one another either. Finding time and money to spend together is our biggest challenge. Something as simple, and inexpensive, as a couch date to talk, cuddle, watch a show, and maybe share a snack is wonderful. Fancy and expensive don't have to be part of a committed, well-functioning parenting relationship.

Babysitters are scarce and pricey for large families and for those with special needs children. We can't just use the teenager down the road to watch our kids. They almost require nursing and psychology degrees to spend ten minutes without killing the one with food allergies or sending the one with autism into meltdown status. We cannot afford even $10 an hour for babysitting, much less the cost of someone who is willing and able to handle the crazy in our home.

We are blessed to have a few friends with whom to trade services. But they have their own children who are also neurodivergent in some way and need their own schedules and routines. And we aren't close to each other geographically. We solve the problem here by putting our younger kids to bed and excusing our older ones from the living room. We commandeer the space and enjoy each other's company. When we have a bit of extra money, we put the little ones to bed and have the older ones watch a movie in the living room so they can watch the dog and keep an ear out for disaster from above. They are also able to address emergencies, know how to talk to Will, and know how to keep Mack safe from his allergens. Until Rory was old enough to stay home alone or with the other kids, we didn't go out except when my parents were in town twice a year. Our couch times became sacred.

Not only do special needs parents have to parent, work, school, and schlepp their kids, but they also have to grocery shop, cook, clean house, and clean people. The workload is impossible even for two adults. Some things can be outsourced. There are some great grocery delivery services available now, like shipt and Instacart. At Your Service does meal planning too. These services can be pricey and aren't available to everyone. Because of the food allergies in our home, we are unable to utilize them.

Sometimes both parents choose to or must work but differ

shifts so there is a parent for schlepping. Others choose to have one parent stay home. For some, like ours, this requires immense sacrifice. For eleven years, we had one vehicle and state insurance. We cook everything at home, which is less expensive than eating out. We buy clothes from thrift stores and love getting hand-me-downs from friends. We don't go on vacations. Other families need both parents working and the jobs don't allow for differing shifts so extended family or bereavement care can help. There are many state programs available to assist families with care of special needs children. There is even state money accessible to subsidize care costs. Some hire full-time nannies or tutors as well. If the family homeschools, then the parents must balance educating their children fully along with all the other demands of general life. When children are in school, stress shifts from constant parenting and educating to managing afterschool breakdowns and homework needs.

A routine is paramount for success. Ability to plan meals for a month or more in advance and have groceries delivered can help a significant amount. Involving children in cleaning the home is also important. Children can alleviate the stress of doing all the housework from the parents and learn the vital life skill of self-sufficiency. Older children can help with younger siblings too. They can help cook some meals. Regular routines for cleaning house and people are critical. From the right child having the right shower at the right time with the right soap and towel to ensuring there is enough hot water to clean the people and the dishes, the routine can get dizzying. Finding the groove that works in your house is important. Shower day in our house is farm day. Everyone who was at the farm takes turns showering as soon as possible after. At least five people shower as a result of farm days. Leigh has his own routine that doesn't interfere with others. And my teen who is in school also has her own needs, which don't run over. Everyone takes turns doing dishes. Everyone folds and puts away their own laundry. Those able also wash and dry their laundry on their own schedules as long as they aren't in the way of my laundry day. We use zone cleaning to clean the whole house once a week. We tidy throughout the week, but the big cleaning happens on Saturdays. Each person gets a zone, which rotates weekly and only repeats once every four weeks. This routine works for us. Our house is decently clean. Our family is happy and well fed.

Siblings

Siblings are always a hot issue. There is so much to balance with siblings of neurodivergent children. We may feel like we are shortchanging "easier" siblings in favor of the "challenging" ones. However, parenting children as individuals is crucial. Each child is different and needs different amounts and kinds of attention. Shifting the paradigm to reflect quality of time rather than quantity of time can be a good way to address this disparity.

Trucking higher needs children to and from doctor visits may feel like we are ignoring other children. We may seek to do the same number of outside-the-house things with our typical children but will simply eat time, and it won't result in quality for anyone. Rather, we should focus on what each child needs in their lives to be successful. One child may thrive in a home education setting for teaching, but another might need private or public schooling. Montessori might be right for another child, while parochial is good for another. It is okay to homeschool one child (or a few) while sending others to school. The best thing is for each child to be in an environment in which they thrive. The best environment is different for each child. A weekly therapy appointment for one, and a weekly swim class for another. Cuddling on the couch and talking over the day might be the medicine needed for one, while another may need a board game or some instructional time.

Allowing our children to determine who they are and what they need is a key part of successfully parenting multiple children. We often remind ours the only reason they should look in another's bowl is to see the other has enough. This simply means they shouldn't compare themselves or the amounts of time they spend with us with each other but should be sure the others have enough proper time. We remind them this with food, privileges, time, etc. We remind them they are different and need different things. We will even ask them whether they really want precisely what a sibling has. The answer is *always* no. But sometimes, they need the reminder we are just as aware of their needs as we are of the needs of the other kids. There are currently five kids under our care. The potential for feelings of jealousy and competition are high. We have to carefully balance each child and ensure their specific needs are being met properly. How we meet needs also tends to change with their ages as their requests change. The neediest one today might be the easiest tomorrow.

We set up a date night with Dad each week. We rotate children through so each has one-on-one time with Dad every fifth week. The child chooses the activity within reason and gets at least an hour with just Dad. They all get me all the time, so we knew dad dates needed to take precedence. After, I arranged our daily schedule to allow each child one-on-one, no-school time with me. The older four children also get to cook dinners with me a week at a time. We spend time talking about life and learning to cook.

Your one-on-one time might be lying in bed and reading in the evening. It might be chats on the way to and from sports or music. Whatever it is, even ten minutes once a week to reconnect can change the dynamic.

Failure is something parents and caregivers of special needs children feel all too often. We feel we are failing our special needs children and our neurotypical ones. We feel we make wrong decisions about practitioners, therapists, schools, extracurricular activities, friends, parties, discipline, and more.

Just this week, I felt like I had, again, failed my son and Leigh. We made the decision to leave our younger three children home so the bigger three and I could quickly do the farm chores and beat a snowstorm home. Unfortunately, Will, had a rough morning that resulted in him losing several privileges including the ability to remain home while Leigh needed to work. His ability to regulate that morning was absent and he terrorized his two younger siblings. If I had been home, he would have been engaged in schoolwork or I would have been able to catch him amping up and been able to separate him from the others. Leigh was working and couldn't quickly assess situations or engage the kids. Had he been with me, he would have been in his normal routine of helping with the horses, which typically goes well. He knows his expectations and generally accomplishes them sans complaint—not that a complaint never happens, but it is rare. Not only did he lose his temper with his siblings, but he retreated to reading rather than accepting and acknowledging fault. He also lost his Kindle and books in general as an escape.

I had been allowing the easy route of him escaping and reading for a time when he was feeling too much, but it became a crutch. Rather than a regulator, it was a true escape from reality. He struggled dealing with the consequences of his actions because rather than work through them and think about them, he was running away. We chose to remove books as an option when he needs time. We are, instead, encouraging meditation and karate patterns. This will, hopefully, help calm his mind and allow him to process rather than ignore his feelings. Then he will be able to converse regarding the incident.

In retrospect, forcing different options for regulation has

helped tremendously. He is permitted books again. The Kindle is his go-to for escaping crowds. At home, he also has meditation, karate, and drumming to help him regain order.

The whole episode left me thinking. Was I doing enough active work with him to help him process his feelings? Was I attentive enough? Was I addressing the cause of his struggles in addition to the symptoms? Did I really need to find him a new therapist more quickly? Had I exhausted all my known coping mechanisms? Had I taught him enough? Was I giving him enough control? Too much control? Was I taking advantage of Leigh?

So many questions race through my mind, and yours too no doubt. We can get caught up in this cycle of doubt so easily. It often leads to depression, which can paralyze. We need the support system of friends, family, and therapists so these times of self-doubt don't get the chance to take over. We need people we can easily talk to about our own feelings of inadequacy. I am certain every parent on the planet feels inadequate every day. I am also certain parents of children who have a high rate of suicide feel inadequate far more intensely. Like everything in our lives, intensity rules. It isn't just children who need support and therapy but the adults who care for them too. I am never endingly thankful for my sister friends who support me unconditionally. And for Leigh, who is my rock. I seriously could not raise these people without their kind of support. Support says, "You're doing great. You might not have handled the situation the best way possible, but I know you are trying, and you love that little boy more than anything!" Support screams, "Have some *wine!*" "And next time, you will do better!"

Sibling Differences

If you're reading this book, you must have at least one person in your life who is neurodivergent. Whether you or a loved one, someone's brain works differently. You might be the parents of multiple children and only one who is gifted. This can present its own set of challenges. Parenting is tough anyway. Then we add neurodivergence. Then toss in some kids are, and others aren't. Parenting this feels like juggling and dropping all the balls. This may be another area in which you feel like you're shortchanging one child while sinking energy into another. We know gifted people have a very different set of intellectual needs. Their basic needs—food, shelter, water, and love—are largely the same. Though they may express love very differently, they still have a distinct need for it. However, their intellectual needs are quite different. Their ability to express their needs varies as well.

Neurotypical children tend to hit certain milestones at relatively predictable times. They crawl a bit after the midpoint of year one. They walk within a month or so of their first birthday. They begin speaking somewhere around age one and gradually increase in their ability to speak coherently. Most children achieve decent speech patterns, including multiple-word, complex sentences and even paragraphs, by around age three. These children tend to understand language and follow simple directions by age two (when they want to, of course). School begins around age five with simple reading and math surrounding letters and numbers that grow in complexity over a long time. Running, jumping, throwing, catching, questions, etc. are all fairly typical and follow a relatively predictable timeline. Sure, there are some outliers with all these milestones for neurotypical children. And there are absolutely the times these children exhaust their parents and are "too much."

There is no typical development for gifted children. None. One will speak within the first six months and be having adult conversations by eighteen months and read by age three (Rory). The next could not utter a single word until after age two and not speak understandably until age four when they could also magically read (Will). Mack was typical for speech development, but his motor development was ridiculous. He rolled over at three weeks of age and crawled at four months. He took off running by nine months. He taught himself to ride a two-wheel bike before he turned six. However, he was more than seven years old before he figured out reading, even though by four he was multiplying. Reading at age seven is perfectly typical, but it demonstrates even in families where everyone is gifted, there are odd development patterns. Nothing is predictable. My fourth is not yet four but is already precocious. She desperately wants to learn to read and write but lacks the focus and fine motor skills for it. She is also a bit clumsy. However, she is a wordsmith like her older sister.

I cannot predict or even anticipate something big is going to happen in one of their brains or bodies because they simply don't follow typical progressions. When they get moody, cranky, whiny, and struggle with regulation, I know something is going on, but I have no way to know what. I can't count on the milestone lists for their ages because they are so all over the map that I can't know what's next. Sometimes I think they've accomplished a milestone only to realize they missed the one immediately preceding it. Will walked before he crawled. He was in turmoil for several months because of his physical developments. When he walked, we wondered if he would skip crawling all together only for him to crawl a month later.

If there are neurotypical and neurodivergent children in the home, the struggle can be even more because they may hit similar milestones simultaneously or jump back and forth with progression. The difficulty is with one being somewhat linear and the other being completely random. We might fill in those baby books right along the lines for one child and have to go back at age five to enter in the ability to follow multistep directions. The two may communicate completely differently too. In my experience with neurotypical children, I need short, simple explanations. This is vastly different from the neurodivergent kids I am around. They require complicated monologues and still don't accept the explanation. Nothing is ever enough. I have had to assert myself far more with my neurodivergent tribe than I ever had to with the neurotypicals I have taught. Even with my strikingly different children, I have to remember whom I am speaking with, so I can ensure my tone and instructions are appropriate. I may be able to quickly tell my oldest she needs to do something (she is gifted in maturity too—most of the time), but I have to ensure eye contact and focus from Mack and have him repeat the steps to me to be certain the job will be accomplished. With Will, I have to give a five-minute warning that I plan on asking him to do something different from what he is already doing lest I face a meltdown. I can ask Kae to do anything at any time and she will tell me no every time. I have to go armed to fight her and convince her clothing is a great idea in subzero temperatures.

We all want to do what's right for our individual children. This is a confusing undertaking. On the one hand, we need to be sure we are treating our children fairly, which may feel like we need to treat them equally. On the other hand, our children are different humans and recognizing their differences and treating them accordingly is appropriate. "Different but equal" is not only a justification for a terrible time in our history but also feels like a false dichotomy. Equity is what we need, not equality. Equal means the same things for each person. Equity is giving each individual the specifics they need. So in our parenting, we need to be equitable. I would do a disservice to my children to treat them all the same. They don't need that. They would resent it. Rory doesn't need step-by-step instruction. She never did. Will doesn't either. But he does need transition time. I have to prepare him. Mack needs the step-by-step but not the transition. Most of the time Kae needs gentle instruction and justification and then support to complete a task. I cannot just set her free. But at her age, I could instruct and walk away from the oldest two. So pay attention to who your children are as people and what they respond best to, so you can treat them equitably.

Each neurotypical child is different and has distinct needs and interests as well. It is paramount in parenting to address each child's needs. I really cannot say this enough. Just as we want to be treated as individuals and accepted and celebrated for our differences, so do our children. They, and we, will fail if we do not respect this. Yet when I tell people Will has autism, they expect him to always avoid eye contact (he only does sometimes) and be unable to explain himself adequately. He is in tune with himself. He knows his needs. Limited experience with those with specific neurological differences lulls us into a sense of understanding. Reality is everyone with autism is different. Everyone with anxiety is different. Everyone with ADHD is different. Celebrating their differences exalts them as humans deserving of consideration.

Another challenge with siblings is helping them learn about each other and how to interact. Some people are simple and straightforward to communicate with, while others are more complex. Role-playing situations depicting different challenging circumstances with siblings helps them begin to understand the others' points of view better. Encouraging them to think of how the other might feel can help with communication too. The reflexive listening I mentioned earlier is a helpful tool for teaching people to communicate better. They are required to listen to each other more than to talk. They are required to make meaning from what the other person says, which means they are thinking about it deeply. Generally, we listen to respond. The goal of this practice is to listen to understand. They are two very different things.

Siblings often struggle to work with each other when they're so different. I have a very mature, silly, sarcastic daughter. She's my oldest. Rory was and is easy, really. So we employed some similar tactics with Will. He is a sweet, sensitive, but complicated soul.

He is my child with anxiety and Asperger's. We had to change how we addressed him. We had to teach Rory how to communicate with him. We had to remind her words are literal to him. Sarcasm didn't make sense. Figurative language was challenging. She had to choose her words carefully too. Then we had Mack. He is a charismatic, energetic, free spirit. He really had to practice speaking to his brother calmly and slowly. The boys are now ten and eight and we still have to have them slow down and talk to each other calmly. Having them take time, feel, evaluate, and come back together with a facilitator is useful in helping them hear each other.

Extended Family

Blood is thicker than water is a familiar phrase, leading us to believe blood relatives are more important and lasting than others. Sadly, this isn't always the case. Families who don't support or who argue about a child's diagnosis or treatment plan are difficult to change. Sometimes we must put up significant boundaries.

Beth is going through the struggle of establishing boundaries with judgmental, disrespectful family. One set of grandparents, Grammy and Poppy, bullies the children, Ellie and Allan. They also disrespect my friend. Grammy consistently talks over Beth and accuses Allan of being rude when he stands up for himself in conversation. Poppy plays roughly with Ellie even when she asks him to stop. When Beth has confronted them in the past, they have shrugged off the occurrences as normal grandparent/grandchild behaviors. Beth and her husband, Kenn, are preparing to sit with them to initiate boundaries. Beth knows the conversation could end the relationship, but she is willing to for the safety of her children and her own sanity.

Explaining to family what your child struggles with and how

they can best support you is the first step. Whether they believe you and respect you and your child is their choice. Remaining in any toxic relationship is not healthy for anyone. If family members disparage or ignore your child or you, they are unlikely to adjust their expectations of what the child should do or who they should be. Seeing your child for who they are, meeting them where they are, and addressing them gently is crucial to maintaining some semblance of sanity and happiness. Some families simply refuse to do this. These families need space. These families you might see once a year at a reunion. Or maybe not. Making peace with this is difficult. But necessary.

Cutting ties with family reminds me of the incident wherein my mother-in-law, Kat, accused my son Will of trying to manipulate her into buying him two toys. He was struggling to decide between two but had never asked for both. I yelled at her and assumed our tenure was up. She also accused him of selfishness when he had a meltdown over her physically moving him away from his baby sister. He had to be the grown up and apologize to her. In reality, had she asked him to move, Will would have complied and shared. But she didn't ask. She didn't respect his body. The abuse nearly ended a vacation early.

Boundaries are challenging but needed. They are more so when there are extenuating circumstances involved.

There are incredible families who step up and encourage the parents and children in neurodivergent families. These families embrace the idea that humans are all different and are to be treated as such. They are willing to read books to understand the child better. They are easy. They're there. Always. They'll babysit. They'll run errands. They're not afraid of the kids.

My parents are this type. But they live across the country. So while they're there, they're not there. When they are here, they are willing to babysit, read, work through disruptions, and concede to children's demands for activities. When we see them twice each year, the children are happy to interact. I do not see the same thrill with others.

Then there are the in-between families. The ones you can educate, but not easily. They seem like they want to understand and show up, but they don't know how. These families want to be educated. They want to know how. We sit with them and walk them through what it means to be part of these special people's lives. They want to see what being in their lives means. Our job is to invite them in and teach them the beauty of our children's brains. One of the biggest struggles we need to walk this family through is the difference between a temper tantrum and a meltdown.

A tantrum is an attempt to change the tides of whatever the current situation might be, like screaming to try to get a cookie. When the demand is met, the tears subside. A meltdown, however, is an expression of deep inability to continue life right now. They are not present. They cannot be reached or reasoned with. They need time to collect themselves and return to reality. Usually, when they are finished with the intense emotional expression, they just need some reconnection.

Regardless of the type of family you have, connecting with them about your children is absolutely worth your time. They may surprise you, pleasantly.

The people who argue with you about your child. The people who "don't see a challenge." The people who say theirs is worse. And so many more. You may eliminate these people from your life. You are not required to attend the fights you're invited to. You are not required to justify your child to anyone. And just because someone's diagnosis may be worse clinically doesn't mean yours or your child's is of less value.

This was a hard lesson for me to learn. I took years to learn, and I think I am still struggling. I am pained when people don't find enough value in my son to stick around and love him through the hard stuff. I'm hurt when people want to gloss over his struggles because someone else is worse. The people who say my child's diagnosis isn't real and he seems *normal* do more damage than they know. It stings when they call his diagnoses a meaningless label. I know deep down my son is not *normal*. I came to terms with that long ago. I have embraced the quirky, emotional, loving, brilliant kid he is. It is their loss if they don't embrace him too. It is their loss if they don't embrace your quirky, intense, caring, brilliant child too.

Notes

Chapter 8

Schooling Options and Accommodations

Education is necessary. Today's school model seems lovely. A bunch of kids of similar ages and theoretically similar abilities learning, playing, and growing together day after day sounds great. In theory, the model of children sitting and reading or being taught through lectures, hands on activities, and visual representations sounds effective. Somewhere along the way, the powers that be decided learning needed to be measured. There had to be something to measure as well. Observation wasn't adequate anymore. Tests. Reports. Speeches. All these things, and more, were devised to measure learning. Not only were assessments required, but also something to assess. They developed standard goals to work toward. Which would then be assessed. So now there are a measurable goal and measuring tool that must be administered. If the learning goal isn't met, there are often punitive consequences. Even when the costs aren't punitive, they still exist. Then you put a student with anxiety in the classroom and ask him to achieve a predetermined learning goal and prove it on an assessment, or there will be trouble. This scenario isn't going to go well at all. And in reality, even without the pressure of consequences, students with anxiety often shut down when they think something is being measured.

Even though we home educate, I needed to see where my children were in math after some time off. I needed to see where we needed to practice more. I explained thoroughly this was a no pressure thing and simply was to show me what I needed to help them solidify. Will shut down anyway. He had several meltdowns about the evaluation. I had to repeatedly reassure him this was in no way going to indicate anything except where he needed to practice. Will was still concerned I was going to be mad at him if he got something wrong, so he wasn't trying. It took several hours and several meltdowns, reconnections, and conversations, but he finally completed ten questions. He did half of one of seven pages. Clearly we have a lot left to tackle, but I hope after he knows well this is not about being right. It solidified to me school where he would regularly be assessed on his knowledge or understanding of class material was not a good match. It made me concerned for his college career. He wants to be a paleontologist. He's going to have to take tests to make that happen. Even on his IQ test, he struggled with committing to an answer. His processing caused his actual IQ to be dramatically lower than it truly is. He's a perfectionist. But he is one who shuts down rather than overworks.

People with anxiety, SPD, and/or giftedness are typically more than average. Everything is more. Here we call it being extra. But some days are more extra. We put a little extra on our extra on those days. Like today. Today, Will had five to six major meltdowns as well as at least ten miniature ones. Kae was clingier than normal and far needier and demanding. The two year old I babysit, Jae, is typically pretty wild, but today he had absolutely no hint of self-control. Rory, who is usually even-tempered, had two meltdowns. And Mack was far more out of control than normal. I am thankful outside is an option for these days, but I lack the energy to come up with creative outlets for the extraness we have experienced. Days when I have to manage nearly every aspect of everyone else's day leave me dry. Not typical exhaustion but complete and utter exhaustion for which there is no treatment. This is not a day a good night's sleep or a glass of wine will mend. Nevertheless, tomorrow, I will rise early and start fresh and do the work necessary to safely and hopefully happily bring everyone through the day.

Self-control. This is a big word and a big expectation. It means someone has the ability to control themselves in almost any situation. We ask young kids to do this. We ask them to remember from one moment to the next too. Furthermore, we expect kids who struggle in any task to demonstrate self-control in the area. We ask children who struggle with sensory input. Either too much or too little. They either seek or avoid. We ask that child to control his or her body or to hold it together when presented with an overload of information. If they don't, we punish. I am not suggesting discipline is unnecessary or unacceptable. I am suggesting, however, punishment is not the answer. I have and will continue to take privileges when my Mack struggles with his impulses and ability to follow directions. This certainly seems punitive, but if I allow a child who is struggling to follow directions attend archery classes, someone is likely to be injured, or worse. When I enforce that that same child must remain glued to my side save for sleep and bathroom times, I am no more punishing him than I am me. But this glued time allows me to directly and immediately help him meet his needs in a constructive, healthy manner. I am able to teach him. Sometimes it is only one day. Others, it is a week. Sometimes even a month is necessary. Or more.

Immediately addressing his overwhelm or ridiculous thoughts of wall climbing is paramount in helping him funnel those feelings well. When I walk away to do something like clean, he tends to take advantage of my absence and explode. The staked time means when I go clean, he does too. He doesn't get the chance to explode because I am helping him throughout the day in a much closer way than normal. We go for as long as necessary, and we revisit often.

Self-control also seeps into the anxiety-ridden person having difficulty controlling their responses to everyday stimuli. Sometimes responses can be quite appropriate. We call it a good day. A day without many meltdowns. But other times, the responses can be incredibly explosive. So much so, the outside observer may think there is something physically wrong to elicit that volume, pitch, and length of wailing. There are in-between levels, but not many. However, we expect the child with anxiety to have more good days than *normal* days. We expect fewer meltdowns each day. This isn't how their brains work.

As many types of people as there are in the world, there are almost as many schools. But our special people still don't fit the mold. A few general umbrellas of schools are home, public, private, Montessori, and gifted. Within each of these types of school are even more specifics. Under homeschooling are unschooling, traditional, extensions, dual enrollment, classical conversations, Montessori, online, Charlotte Mason, co-op, and any combination of these. Within public schools, there are charter schools and schools with self-contained gifted or special education classrooms as well as those in which the student is in a mainstream classroom with a time they are pulled out for specialized instruction. Private schools include both religious and nonreligious versions. There are also self-contained Montessori-style schools and gifted academies, sometimes called preparatory schools, which can also be religious.

Homeschool

Unschooling is a form of homeschooling wherein the children direct their learning. There are ranges of this from whole life unschooling to more cooperative and responsive education. In whole-life unschooling, children direct all aspects of their education and life skills learning. Parents, of course, intervene in truly dangerous situations wherein the child would be ill-equipped to decide, like with vehicle safety. The parents answer questions and demonstrate through how they live, but most decisions are up to the child. If your children are driven to learn and do well with being left to discover on their own, this style of schooling and parenting may work quite well for you.

However, for those of us who want a bit more control, unschooling can also look like children being largely in charge of their learning environments, materials, and subjects. Students choose the areas of interest and study, with parental involvement and facilitation, as deeply as they can understand or desire before moving to something else. Anywhere in between those two extremes, families can be found unschooling in life and/or school.

In traditional homeschooling, parents choose a curriculum and follow it with their children. It is quite straightforward. It is similar to school schooling. Students have the comfort of home and absence of many school variables while getting what many parents feel is necessary: a structured schooling experience.

With extensions, the parents can do as they please at home, within state laws, and outsource certain subjects. Students may take math or art from someone other than a parent. They might have a physical education type class organized with students from other types of school environments.

There is also dual enrollment wherein a student may take classes at home and at a public or private school. Sometimes the additional courses are at a local community college. This is similar to extensions, but typically this involves more core classes like math and science while the expansion is typically extracurricular, though it can involve core classes as well.

Classical conversations and Charlotte Mason are two of many specific styles of curriculum models. These two are strict in their requirements and procedures. Others are less so. There is a wealth of information available online regarding these and other methods.

Online schooling is much what it sounds like. There are several online, complete public school experiences students can participate in from home. Students log into an online portal where they access assignments, teacher lectures, classroom discussions, tutoring, assessments, and more. They are evaluated through this system according to the state's standards. Parents have to facilitate this only slightly by logging hours of off-screen work and occasionally grading an off-screen assignment.

Co-ops are cooperative endeavors among homeschool families. In this situation, students attend classes in a common building but in separate classrooms. The parents are the teachers, but they each teach a subject or two in which they are experts while their children learn from other parents who are experts in other fields.

Public School

Public school is any school available to a child free of charge. The government requires free, public education to all children. The government in turn oversees these schools and requires certain outcomes. The measuring sticks are standardized tests that every school in the nation must complete. There are variations regarding how and when certain tests are administered, but they communicate efficacy of the school and determine funding. Each school must also adhere to certain benchmarks regarding what students learn at different times or ages. How the concepts are taught varies state to state and teacher to teacher.

There aren't as many variations on types of public school options. Montessori schools are sometimes included in the general umbrella but are still subject to the state and federal specifications for curriculum. As they are subsidized or entirely paid for by the state government, the schools must still report student progress. Montessori schools enact the curriculum differently in an attempt to follow the methods put forth by Maria Montessori in her Casa di Bambini. She purported that students would fare better when left to their own interests. Her model took hold across the world, though still isn't implemented consistently.

Private School

Private schools are those one must pay for. They are often parochial, but some are secular. Though the private citizen pays for their children to attend private schools, they are still held to a standard as they must compete on a national level. Often private schools are more rigid with structure and expectations. They also have more freedom with curriculum implementation. Private schools are not accessible for a majority of families because the cost per semester is typically upward of $4,000.

No matter what type of school works best for your child, there still may be some hurdles to face. There are further accommodations available for individuals depending on their needs. These include IEP, 504, paraprofessionals or aides, pull-out time, special education or gifted-only rooms, and mainstream rooms with any or all the above assistance. Testing accommodations are also possible and are often detailed in the IEP or 504. Sometimes tests may be dictated, students may have extended time on tests, or they may have private testing to remove all potential distractions.

An IEP is an individualized education plan that outlines specific needs of the student and the accommodations necessary to create the least restrictive environment. Parents or teachers may request the IEP meeting. The gathering includes the classroom teacher, parents, principal, and resource teacher or school psychologist. The group decides whether a student would benefit from assistance and what kind is necessary. After the IEP is agreed upon and written, the teacher must implement the plan fully and without wavering. The agreement and implantation are the most challenging portions of the IEP. Parents and teachers don't often agree on necessary accommodations for the student and the school may lack funds to pay for the needed adjustments. Implementation is a challenge as a single classroom teacher must now assist potentially three or more students in a classroom of more than twenty-five.

A 504 is similar to an IEP in both accommodate the student and attempt to achieve the least restrictive environment. However, the 504 covers more than the thirteen specific conditions listed for IEP. The 504 can help those with food allergies or who are wheelchair bound where the IEP is specifically for those with learning outcome related struggles.

Regardless of what schooling route you choose, there are bound to be transition times to contend with. Starting school, school breaks, and returning after school breaks. Even if you choose to homeschool year-round or unschool, there are times when the general routine is upset. These are times our little brains do not handle terribly well. Prepping them for the coming change can help tremendously. Setting the expectation for what their lives will look like during the different period can help too. Writing out schedules and doing a countdown to return to normalcy can alleviate some of the stress too.

Perhaps the biggest disrupters are starting school, Christmas break, and summer break. These things seem to happen just when children have securely settled into their new routines and are going along quite well. Then we yank them out of routine, thrust them into something different only for a short time, just to throw them back to the old routine. It sounds terrible. I can only imagine the feelings of frustration and confusion these children feel about the upheaval. Taking away just some of the stress they feel is positive. We know routine and expectation are important. Whatever we can do to maintain something similar to a consistent routine and clearly explain the changes will help.

Parent Stories

I asked in several Facebook based support groups for parental stories about school and the way they made their decisions for their neurodivergent children. Here they are verbatim:

Parent 1: Our local school district is inconsistent based on the principals. When my 2e son (gifted plus very significant medical problems that prevented him from ever attending school more than three hours a day) got to middle school, the principal flat out said no to his IEP even with the district reps and advocate from the hospital present. After the meeting, we decided we had to withdraw him for his safety. His health is so fragile that we couldn't risk it during the fight. We were never even able to address his gifted education at all.

Parent 2: My background is law. I left practice to stay home with my kids (so even as a family who is privileged to afford a homeschooling lifestyle, the financial loss is profound). After hearing so many stories, I decided a few years back to start a niche practice focusing on special education. Long story short, the demand was so great, even in my rural community, that I was overwhelmed within weeks and eventually made the decision to focus on my own child's needs because I couldn't do both well! It's hard for families with the funds and advantages; it's nearly impossible for those lacking either.

Parent 3: I completely understand. We still rent a home because we haven't been able to afford buying one on one salary. But at least we make do. So many families can't even if they wanted to. There's gotta be a better public solution for accelerated learners. I read somewhere this philosophical question: "Is a cheetah still a cheetah if it's enclosed in too small of a space that it can never reach its top speed?" It related this to gifted children in the American education system. Every child should be able to learn at their speed. Personally, I always thought a lot of this could be fixed with skill-based rather than age-based classes.

Parent 4: We got tested for 2E yesterday and will have results next week. The new principal came from a public school program with a very good gifted and SPED program (separate). They asked for the cognitive test to better serve him. We are in a smaller private school with 5 percent IEP kiddos.

Parent 5: My son is thirteen, HG, atypical ADHD, SPD, two years accelerated (one year by his school, one by me). We started in a rigorous curriculum/very conventional school setting where we dealt with meltdowns and behavioral issues, especially in grade 2. After an ASD eval, we were advised about the SPD, high IQ, and slow processing speed (technically no ASD but he'd tick every box if Asperger's was still a diagnosis). The evaluators' recommendation was a different school (ideally for gifted kids). Those are in short supply, but we found a STEM school he attended in grades 3–7 (skipped sixth by his teacher) and again began having issues due to lack of engagement/sensory issues, etc. Implemented a 504 with accommodations for extended time on tests, sensory breaks, clarification of instruction, etc. Had a WISC-V performed after talking to a gifted advocate and at her recommendation accelerated again into an area high school with a gifted magnet program. This involved an hour of social/

emotional support built into every day and supposedly many other supports. The program was great but lacked the resources to do all that was advertised. Sensory was a huge issue at the school, as was 504 adherence, and organizational deficits made semester 1 a struggle. Finally a behavioral issue and a suspension drove us to look elsewhere. Semester 2 at a smaller charter was catastrophic with lots of bullying and again *tons* of issues with 504 adherence. Began looking into online school, found one in a neighboring district (the same district with the magnet program), and my kiddo is now enrolled. While not perfect, it's been a much better match, especially since I can help support executive functioning issues around organization and there's a built-in accounting of all assignments. (I should mention I work from home and have a *very* flexible job, which makes this feasible.) Teachers have been highly supportive and incredibly communicative, have offered solutions when there were struggles, and have largely ignited a passion for learning in him again. It's hard for everyone. I'd definitely make different decisions in hindsight, but I think we've finally found our match and an educational model that works for him. If you need a count, this is school five in the nine years since it started.

Parent 6: My son does online public school. He is 2e (ADHD, autism, and gifted) and has an IEP and 504 plan. He has one hour of OT a week through the school. This helps him with his writing and concentration. He has skipped a grade and has extra enrichment for math. The online school has a gifted program to help as well. He struggles with writing and will have meltdowns when he needs to do papers for school. I am working to get him bumped up another grade in math, but I have to go through multiple time-consuming channels to get there. When he was in pre-K and kindergarten in brick and mortar school, we struggled with their concern about maturity and ability to sit still when it came to advancing him into classes that were on his educational level. He would get suspended multiple times, and his relationship with other students was strained. The teachers tried to give him enrichment in the classroom, but they expected him to do it while the rest of the class was listening to the teacher. This was distracting and isolating.

Parent 7: Our eldest attended public until grade 3. She was allowed to grade-split kindergarten and first (at our request) and was screened for the GT program. The district (very large) screened all K kids for GT, then placed them in cluster classes (ability grouping) beginning in first. There was also a weekly pull-out program. We then had her tested to skip first grade, so she was able to attend second, then third. In second, she began having anxiety issues. (We didn't know it at the time; we just knew she cried often at school.) The teacher tried to accommodate her need for continued acceleration but did not have time. The weekly GT pull-out happened *maybe* monthly. At that point, we began researching homeschooling. In grade 3, six weeks in, we talked with the principal. My father was not allowed to work ahead in math or to supplement math at school because it was the first year of standardized testing. She offered another grade skip to fourth. She also said they may not be able to accommodate our daughter because she was accelerated in all areas, not just one area, as was typical with most gifted kids. Simultaneously, we had a kindergarten-aged son who was looking like he was also going to need grade skipping. At that point, we pulled them to homeschool. My daughter's anxiety lessened considerably once she'd been home for a while. As a teen, it's resurfaced, but we are better able to recognize and deal with it since she's older and communicates better. She also has some sensory issues (aural and physical) that are either surfacing or she's finally communicating. My son may have something mild with his writing, and he has an odd form of color blindness, but neither kid has a 2e diagnosis. They are just a little odd sometimes and a whole lot of themselves. They are currently sixteen and fourteen, and we've used everything under the sun to school, including unschooling. Right now, they do some things at home, online, and as dual credit at the local CC. I don't really teach, but I facilitate.

Parent 8: My oldest is PG but very asynchronous. We got early entrance to a K program through a local Catholic school, but he was working years ahead in math. They very lovingly told us that they didn't have the resources to meet his advanced needs. He got into a charter school for gifted children. We were there for two years, and it was pretty amazing. We moved to California, where the options were limited. We attended a public school that was considered one of the best in the country. They have a small gate full-time program that is highly competitive based on CoGat scores. My son didn't make it and most likely wouldn't have been successful in it. It is geared toward high achievers. During the school year, my oldest was bullied intensely. We had many, many trips to the principal. He is most likely 2e but has no specific diagnosis (yet).

Enter child 2. He is also PG and 2e. He has several dysgraphia, stealth dyslexia, and auditory processing disorder. School was torture for him. He never failed enough to need services so never got the supports needed. I was spending upward of twenty hours a week just on their homework, advocacy, volunteering, etc. It just made sense to bring them home. I also have a little one who is just now starting K. I can work with my kids by letting my fourth grader be in prealgebra and also enrolling him in social skills classes. My second grader can type all of his lessons. I can find tactile math to teach concepts. The flexibility in curriculum is what has sold me on homeschooling.

Parent 9: Homeschool and online college courses. Public school bored him out of his mind, and his teacher wanted him drugged because of his high level of motivation. He is 2E, but in a classroom all that could be seen was how poorly he fit into that setting. The counselor suggested I pull him for his own safety. The school was very overfull, and there wasn't much they could do about other kids targeting and assaulting him. We did have a 504 starting in fifth grade, but some middle school teachers refused to follow it. It was really disappointing and dangerous.

Parent 10: Big question! Abbreviated answer: three public schools, two of them G&T in name but not actuality. Given the runaround regarding needed supports (writing, social-emotional). Refusal to differentiate/accelerate/compact curriculum. DS8 turns out to be profoundly gifted and ASD1. Now going to private school for 2E kids. Only three days in. He's much happier, more flexible, etc. It's the first time I feel he's safe at school (from emotional abuse from teachers who don't get it and bullying from other kids, which seemed to just be starting in second grade). I'm hoping he'll be academically challenged for the first time too. That's the promise anyway.

Parent 11: My story is easy. Where we live, they don't even test children for giftedness because they have *nothing* for gifted students. They can either bump kids up a grade (my child is doing math 6 grade levels ahead of his age) or make them the teacher's assistant (grading others' worksheets to keep them busy). Neither of those options was acceptable to me. For kindergarten, we sent our son to the local private school that teaches one grade level above the public schools. Despite frequent meetings with the teacher and principal, they just didn't seem to honor the knowledge our son already had, and they kept giving him busywork. We realized that he has learned what he's learned through play and asking questions, and school just took up seven valuable hours each day. We are giving him back that space and time to learn at his own pace. We do fifteen minutes of math every day (Smartick), and he reads *Calvin and Hobbes* after bed for an hour every night. (On his own, we gave him a reading light and gave him freedom to stay up as late as he wants so long as he stays in bed.) Other than that, he asks questions and we answer them or show him how to find the answers. With breakfast, the kids are watching a YouTube video about human gestation because they wanted to know how babies are formed. (This started with the three year old asking, "Can dads make babies?")

Parent 12: We did Christian schools for my oldest: K and first. She is MG and academically was at the top of her class but doing fine, just distracted constantly by wanting to be social. So socially it wasn't my favorite for her. When my younger one, DD6, was identified as PG (at age four by the public school district we had just moved into), we had her and my older one enrolled in a new Christian school, and I got a bad feeling when we'd talk to admins there about our situation with DD4. The public school district had accelerated DD4 into first grade (skipping kindergarten), but the private school seemed still very hesitant in wanting to "accommodate" a girl who is PG. And they also seemed hesitant to even believe she was PG even *after* we had test scores to prove it. I realized this would be an uphill battle with every new teacher each year, so she never even started there, and we chose to homeschool both girls. It's been working out beautifully. I have no complaints now, but it is still really disappointing how teachers are so resistant to wanting to "deal with" kids who are advanced! I get it though. They have way too many kids who are behind to make it a priority, and that's just the reality. We also have a DD3. She's similar in many ways to my PG DD6, but we really don't know her "status" and aren't worried about it. We'll be homeschooling her regardless so there's much less to worry about.

Parent 13: We have PG/2e nine year old, likely HG seven year old, no idea yet five year old, and also likely PG two year old. We tried public school for kindergarten and first with our oldest. She hid everything she knew to fit in in kindergarten. It was only half a day, so we were able to just let her go have fun in the morning with the other kids and then fill her thirst for learning in the afternoon. So it worked. First grade was a disaster. We went up there several times to try to get help but were told services didn't start until third grade and the teacher would put her in a reading group with other higher-level readers who turned out to be kids doing second semester reading. They were not willing to work with her in any other way and said she didn't qualify for special early testing because she was doing just fine. She became a mess, so we pulled her before the end of the first nine weeks.

We have an awesome online public charter school here in Oklahoma, so we tried that instead of doing straight homeschooling, and it's working great! Since the kids test high, they let us do anything we want. It's literally like we homeschool except we have testing and everything we want to do is paid for. So through that program, we order whatever level of curriculum we need for each subject and work through it at whatever pace we want. We do compacting, explore topics more in depth, and go for higher grade levels. Up until this year, this has let us keep each kid in their age grade, which has been nice. This year we pursued a formal skip with the oldest, because she wants to go to the enterprise school Leigh teaches in for middle school. It is application only, with test scores being the criteria, and they do "advanced" work with lots of project-based learning and standards-based grading, which means they move on according to whether they've mastered the material. We knew she would need to go a year early though for it to still be a good fit, so we went ahead and skipped her. The school was eager to work with us, and the process was simple. She just had to score at the 95 percentile on their benchmark testing and complete the work for the grade she was "skipping" in their test prep program to show she knew the material. I suspect it will be a similar course with the younger kids.

I hope these stories give you all some encouragement and necessary information about your choices too. And help you see the decision of how to educate these special children is not an easy one and often comes through trial and error.

Teachers

Teaching is one of the biggest, most thankless jobs there is. They work tirelessly trying to match government standards with student learning ability and style. But they do this with thirty or more students daily. It is simply not possible to meet every need for every student. I know they try. Most of the time.

Teachers and parents need to work together to ensure the best education possible for our neurodivergent children. This is a big call. And one that seems all but impossible to answer. Parents and teachers must work together to do so.

First, parents, we need to talk to the teachers. We need to inform them about who our precocious students are and how they thrive. Then we need to back up the information with help. These teachers have many students with different needs. We can't be helpful if we tell a teacher our child needs extra then walk away and not help provide the extra. The teacher already has an overfull plate. You probably do too, but together, you can share the load. Help the teacher out with what will make your child's heart love learning—if you know.

Teachers, listen to the parents. I know you hear constantly Johnny is gifted and needs extra help. I heard it all the time when I taught. But I am also certain it takes a week or two for you to pin down who is really different. When a parent brings you a stack of papers from the psychologist and looks haggard and desperate, they probably aren't tooting their child's horn too much. That parent probably does desperately need help. This child will probably thrive in your classroom if you take a few extra steps toward helping them learn deeply. Let them read the more challenging books. Encourage harder math. Pull resources from upper grade teachers to deepen their sciences and social studies needs. Modify assignments to allow them to delve deeper into the subject matter.

All this can be done with the aid of the parents. But don't hesitate to encourage their love. Also, don't ask them to teach the other students. Teaching others isn't fair to them. The neurodivergent students deserve their own stimulation. Teaching something you already know to someone struggling to learn it isn't the kind of brain growth these students need or deserve.

When you have students struggling with autism or anxiety, really listen to their parents about what and how to speak to them to get them engaged in something they resist. Talk to the student too, if they are able, and listen to what they say about how they prefer to learn. Will needs a schedule. If the schedule is going to be deviated from, he needs warning and recovery time. Students with anxiety and autism, among other things, struggle with surprises. Whenever possible, warn them about changes and drills. Pop quizzes and surprise tests are scary too, so a bit of warning can be good. I am not saying eliminate the surprise entirely, but maybe let them know earlier in the day so they can mentally prepare. Or change the wording to indicate you're looking simply for what is understood now so you know where to go and where students are struggling.

You may have students who are disruptive in some manner. They may need to move while listening or doing their work. They may need redirection or reminders now isn't the time to chat. They may need strategic desk placement. They may need more frequent breaks in the day. These are all things that don't disrupt their learning or the learning of others.

Howard Gardner studied how children learn and settled on <u>Seven Intelligences</u>. It is possible and even likely to do well with more than one of these learning and teaching methods. What is important is knowing which and understanding how to implement them for ourselves and our children.

The seven basic intelligences are logical-mathematics, linguistic-verbal, visual-spatial, musical, bodily-kinesthetic, intrapersonal and interpersonal. Some of these are obvious per the name—logical-mathematical learners learn sequentially and through patterns and generally enjoy sciences and math. Linguistic learners are more language driven, learning through manipulation of language. Spatial learners tend to create and change mental images to enhance learning and is often found in blind children who must rely on visualization to create images of things they cannot see. In musical learners, pitch and tone help solidify learning. Bodily-kinesthetic learners tend to need to move while learning and can enhance their learning when they are able to put it in motion. Intrapersonal learners are aware of their own emotional states, and frequently use introspection to aide their learning. Finally, interpersonal learners understand the feelings and intentions of others and themselves and can use their relationships with people and information to learn.

Discovering our children's intelligences can open doors to their drive to learn new information and assimilate old information. We can create beautiful learning environments when we pay attention to their needs and answer them. Teaching the way students learn is crucial to student success. This goes beyond the classroom too and into life. Our children may have huge aspirations that require several of the intelligences. By incorporating their goals and passions with their learning styles, we empower them to truly achieve greatness.

I know one plight of classroom teachers is students observe different treatment of other students and decide they need some special treatment too. Teachers must combat the feelings of unfairness daily. One way to do so is to be clear you are trying to achieve the least restrictive, most successful learning environment for all students. Provided work is being completed to the best of a student's ability and they are working to learn, the environment can be flexible for them too. Encourage students to explore how they learn best. Some students may prefer sitting in desks and working diligently and silently. Others may benefit from sitting on exercise balls or bean bag chairs. These things can be pricey and school budgets certainly don't cover them. Teachers already spend a large portion of their own money to furnish classrooms with things like pencils and paper. Parents can help provide these flexible seating options for the classroom or for the student to carry through grades with them.

Ultimately, a positive relationship among teacher, learner, and parent can be reached when all parties listen to each other for the purpose of listening and truly hearing and with a goal of helping everyone succeed. Parents and teachers should be allies in helping students gain the learning they wish to gain.

Notes

Chapter 9

Tough Subjects

I have talked about the depth and extraness of how our kids process the world. School is challenging because they struggle with the perfunctory nature of the typical classroom. They have deep thoughts and questions about life and the world around them. Will experiences the world more deeply than I have witnessed before. Rory is thoughtful and ponders life. Mack rushes through like a truck but doesn't miss a beat. Kae considered our very existence, saying, "I just don't know why we're here." She is three. Simple concepts don't exist. Difficult concepts become more complex.

Religion

In the United States, there are over three hundred religions. In a country with a population of more than 320 million, around 77 percent of people observe a religion. With religion comes certain expectations. Neurodiverse people tend to struggle to accept and practice norms like this. They often have deep theological questions. Along with needing to learn social customs, we expect these kids to learn social religious customs without clear answers. There are as many interpretations of the Bible as there are people who follow it. The same is likely true of the holy texts from other religions. The Torah, Bhagavat Gita, Quran, Book of Mormon, and many more have followers of varying ethnicities, cultural backgrounds, socioeconomic statuses, family structures, etc. We cannot fathom the depth of thought some people experience regarding these and other open texts. Students of theology remain students until they can no longer learn: at death. There is no end. So for people who operate in the concrete and for whom abstract thought is challenging, the belief there is no answer can seem impossible. Yet parents expect kids to accept their religious belief systems openly and exclusively. Or we expect them to come to their own conclusion, which we hope matches ours. Further struggles arise when kids ask questions their parents cannot answer. More so, when kids probe into aspects parents don't want to consider or they strongly disagree with.

This is a touchy area for many families who feel very strongly about the conclusions they've arrived at regarding religion. Their children challenge them to deeper thought and understanding, but they also challenge something very personal. Walking away from a deeply held personal belief system and culture can be painful. What we need to realize is our children aren't asking us to betray our beliefs. They are requesting that we explain in a more tangible manner. This is also a challenge. We often believe things we cannot explain.

My method for combatting this struggle is to read the holy text of the familial religion slowly. During which time, we can have open and honest communication regarding their thoughts and feelings. Understanding these people are simply asking for more information can help us step back and become less defensive. We need to remember they are not attacking our cultures but understanding them.

When our kids come to us with deep questions, we try to ask them about their thoughts and feelings before inserting our own. We ask them how and why they feel as they do. After we have helped them explore and engage in their own beliefs, we share our feelings on the topic. While we aren't trying to change their ideas, we are teaching them how to have a conversation with someone who may disagree with them. Will and Rory have both researched old and young earth views from biblical and scientific standpoints. They have arrived at opposite conclusions, though both still believe there was a catalyst to earth's creation and call the catalyst God. Leigh and I actually land on opposite sides of this particular discussion too. We each have a child who agrees with us and one who doesn't. Neither of us feels betrayed. We feel accomplished our kids feel free to make their own choices and discuss them with us.

Death

Our precious deep thinkers. Death, as religion, is not simple. Death is permanent. Often there isn't prevention. Sometimes it is sudden. Regardless, it must be handled. Dealt with. Explained. Commiserated. And probably dwelt on for years after.

Since we work on a farm, we see life created and ended regularly. We lost ducks last year. These weren't cuddly, snuggly ducks we bonded with. Yet my son wept over their untimely deaths. Our pig also died suddenly. Cue more big tears. Even worse, his favorite horse, the one he bonded with immediately. The one he loved. The first one he rode. The one who came when he called. He had to be put down because of old age and illness. Euthanasia was the humane thing to do. It was the loving thing to do. He understood the logic. But his precious heart broke. Will's heart continues to break over two years later. He still cries to me about his best friend. He wakes at night thinking of the horse he loved.

He has another best horse. But his new love will never replace his old love. And sadly, the new horse isn't new. So he too would not live much longer. I struggle with whether to remind him sometimes this horse will also be dying soon. Or to just let them enjoy each other with however long there is left. Yet I don't decide when the horse goes. I get no opinion in the matter. I know my son does better when he is able to prepare and ponder and hug and think. I know he will want to spend more time with the horse leading up to the day. I know he will struggle regardless. And unfortunately, all this recently came to fruition. We're again holding his heart as he mourns another death.

I know I am talking about animals here, and people are different. My son hasn't lost any people he is truly close to. Sure, he has been to funerals. He understands the finality of death. He has seen his father and me mourn the loss of loved ones. But it has yet to be someone he truly loved. He is close to so few people. People are hard. Animals are easier. When our little ones bond, be it with humans, animals, toys, or ideas, they bond *hard*. The bond is not easily broken. Even through death. So when our babies lose those they love, they take it hard.

All we can realistically do is hug them when they need. Be there to listen. Not fix. Just listen. And hug. We explain as simply as possible. Answer their questions honestly and lovingly. Hold them. If they are in counseling, letting the counselor know about the loss is also important. Encourage them to talk about their feelings or write their feelings. No pressure. Just reminders we are there for them when and how they need us to be.

Most important is our understanding this type of permanent loss is going to affect them bigger and more deeply than someone else. We should be prepared for more questions of mortality and what happens after death too. These things can be difficult to answer. Especially if we are also grieving. Being gentle with ourselves and our children (and spouses) is crucial. Not easy but crucial. Family counseling can help too. Death is hard regardless of how your brain works. Support and love are how any of us survives loss.

Injustice/World Violence/Events

Our world is rife with injustices. Simple events like a sibling getting a slightly larger piece of pie to massive inequality like slavery and apartheid. While we need to walk carefully along the lines of educating our children on these events, we must not shelter them either. We must prepare our young hearts and minds for the realities of the world while they can still crumble into our laps for comfort and reassurance. We have to walk with them as they discover how awful the world can be so we can teach them to handle it. I am not talking about *toughening* them up against feeling life. But suggesting we teach them how to navigate the very appropriate feelings they will experience.

Will is my most sensitive, but all my children have deep love and concern for the creatures of this world. Will has a heart for people who have less than him. No house. No hair. No food. These hit him deeply, and he wants to share. Many neurodivergent children feel and question deeply about the world at large. They don't understand why people mistreat others but need there to be a more concrete explanation. Will needs to control his world, and we are working with him on flexibility when he can't. But the mistreatment of others is a struggle for him to accept.

Rory shares Will's love for humans but also for animals. Her heart for our furry friends drove her to choose vegetarianism. She can't bear the thought of being responsible for the death of any creature. They share the desire to rescue people too. Rory has a dear friend who struggles with anxiety and self-harm. She wants to be Lyd's rock—always available and supportive. Will wants desperately to provide for those without. Mack and Kae love people, which shows in their interactions. Though neither has a desire or need to save others yet, they love profoundly.

We have to talk with our kids about school shootings, bombings, war, and more. We must teach them how to feel and navigate these terrible events while we are there to catch them. We have to answer their questions about why people do terrible things to one another. We cannot allow them to grow up blind to the world. They will fall and fail if we don't hold them up while we teach them now.

Leigh and I are tasked with raising their hearts to adults who can adore the world and its people. Just as you are tasked with aiding the emotional development of your children. When we talk about the cruelty of the world openly, we demonstrate our own feelings. We don't hesitate to cry about what affects us deeply. We don't stop at talk. We demonstrate conversation. We brainstorm how we can realistically help. Paramount among those is kindness. We try to be kind to all those we meet. We don't know who has lost a parent in the last week. We don't know who is struggling with self-doubt in their new job. We don't know who is healing from trauma of any kind. We are kind.

First and foremost, we are honest with our children when they ask us questions. Even when we don't know, we are honest. We work through feelings and events side by side. Our kids are going to ask the really hard questions, and we will have to face our own insecurities about the answers. The best thing we can do for our kids is to be open, raw, and honest. Many of our kids will also become emotionally distraught with injustice. We need to be there for them in whatever capacity is necessary.

Sexuality

Many neurodivergent kids explore life more deeply than their peers. This will include questions of sexuality and reproduction earlier than parents like to broach the topics. When I was pregnant with Will, Rory, not yet two, asked me more than I was prepared to answer at that point. I was thankful I had an illustrated book about the formation of mammals that didn't include a how-to guide. Her questions were innocent, and I answered only exactly what she asked. We didn't have to talk about intercourse specifics. She was happy knowing that daddies have sperm and mommies have eggs and when they join, babies begin to form. To this day, she hasn't asked how the two get together, so I'm sure she figured it out on her own. Just like with most of life. Don't worry. The lines of communication are still open.

As with all our parenting, honesty and straightforwardness are important. We answer specifically any question they throw at us. Rarely, we decide they aren't ready for the complexity of the full answer, so we answer in part and tell them there is more, but they aren't ready so we will hold onto the rest until they are.

Our society is rife with people who believe and act differently. Included in that diversity are those whose relationships look different from Leigh's and mine. We are cisgender, heterosexual, monogamous, married-before-children people. My parents are as well. Leigh's parents were divorced when he was ten. Both remarried at some point. Their relationships were different. Rory has several friends whose parents are experiencing divorces. Two of our six exchange students had parents with solid single marriages. All these people are cisgender and heterosexual. However, we do have people in our lives who are gender fluid, exploring, bisexual, or homosexual. Our children know. As often as they have asked deep questions about relationships, this is one area they accept at face value. Two people love themselves and each other. End of story. Their only questions come from the words used to describe different people and whether the terms are kind or not.

Rory is at an age during which children begin to explore their own sexuality and place in the world. Rory isn't questioning her own yet, but I have no doubt her friends are and are talking to her about their own considerations and crushes. Rory has agreed to come to us with thoughts and questions. I hope she does. She has seen us address our teen students with their questions, so she knows we are gentle and nonjudgmental. She hears us discuss sex as a contract of love between two people that is not to be taken lightly. She hears us talk about respect in a relationship. She hears us urge thoughtfulness.

Will and Leigh are going to spend a lot of time talking about how to hold relationships with other people when your brain functions as theirs do. Leigh had a difficult childhood without this conversation, but he doesn't want his children to miss out on the benefit of involved parents. Mack has already had admonishment about respecting others' bodies, as have they all. But Mack more so with his need to touch. He knows he needs permission to touch others.

Notes

Chapter 10

Beginners' Guide to Raising Neurodivergent Children

You will never know or be able to predict what's next. Just when you think you have your child's triggers figured out, they will throw you a curveball. This will be the hardest job with the longest hours. You will rarely meet people in real life who have kids like yours or who truly understand you. You will begin to understand yourself better than you thought possible. You will be challenged in ways you never knew existed. Even if you've never before been speechless, you will experience the feeling because of something your child does or says. You will find yourself shaking your head in disbelief regularly. You will spend more time, money, and energy on cracking the code of raising these children than you realized imaginable. You will become friends with coffee, strong tea, chocolate, or some other vice to help you connect with yourself after another long day.

Don't be scared. This is also the most invigorating journey you will ever embark on. You will see more glorious sights and breathe in more miraculous discoveries than contained in all the wonders of the world. These children are a blessing larger than life itself. There is no comparison with the intensity of their desires to learn or your love for them. They will show you truths about life you have never pondered. There will never be a dull moment. They will keep you on your toes constantly. This will be the most fulfilling time of your life, and you will be better for it.

Now that we have the feelings out of the way, let's get practical. These neurodivergent toddlers are not going to be hoodwinked by the typical toddler tricks. They will figure out a way around them. You will feel bested by your toddlers. Even as infants, they are likely to be different. More intense somehow. Not necessarily more crying or difficult, just intense. Will was content to sit and observe life, but his eyes were deep and soulful. He was learning about life before he even really lived any. Mack never sat still—*ever*. He was more interested in learning how to move and manipulate existence than how it worked. My girls were different still. Rory learned then demonstrated life through writing and drawing. Kae observed being and needs to move it and talk about it.

Regardless of their personalities, we saw they needed different parenting than their peers had. I actually could use logic with my toddlers. Well, with three of them. With Mack, I needed brute force because he took the logic and thought he could break it and create new logic. He is the one who, at age two, figured out how his bike worked by observing it standing still, then explained the mechanics to me. He was not to be told how anything worked. When I could, I let him figure it out for himself. This led to people really judging me on the playground. My very able, very stubborn two year old was climbing things the five and six year olds struggled with. The other moms tried to help him to be met with screams of "No! Myself!" Then they looked at me. I ceremoniously stood near him so others would at least think I was the attentive parent I am. But I knew he didn't need me. The rare times others commiserated with me, I felt validated in my hands-off approach to this child. There will always be outside observers who silently (or not so silently) judge your parenting. *Please* wrap yourself in the knowledge you *know* this child and you're parenting according to his needs rather than the needs some bystander thinks you should be.

Those outside observers who don't know your child will also judge you when you appear to coddle your older child when they break down over what they think is the smallest thing. Don't stop answering the cries of your double-digit children because others think they're too old to cry over hurt feelings or missed expectations. Those emotions and needs are as big as they were when the child was two. Keep parenting *your* children, parents. Don't let others make you feel less somehow because your kid is more. When you have to drag your very emotional toddler out of a store and force them into the car seat, remember this child is feeling bigger than the world right now. You are not being unkind if you're not able to take the time right now to hug through the emotions of leaving a favorite place. You may leave even when the child isn't ready. You probably gave fifteen countdown warnings already. You can't speed them up. You can hug them and speak reassuring words about their feelings. You can assure yourself and your child that sadness and crying are okay. Then carry on with what you need to do to get everyone safely out of the store and into the car. If one of those bystanders is sympathetic and offers help, accept. The offer of help is rare. But chances are they understand. Understanding is rarer.

Equally as judgmental are those who observe your newly minted three year old reading the tabloids in the checkout aisle. Yes, she can read. Yes, those are eye level. Yes, she knows what those words mean. No, you shouldn't question my child's reading ability. You should question the placement of the tabloids. Also, don't get offended when she uses a big word then defines it to an adult. She knows what she knows but not what you know. Just laugh and nod your head. She isn't trying to offend.

People will judge your parenting from the outside, tiny snippets they see. Remember you have been parenting these children and know what makes them tick *most* of the time. And you know, sometimes, how to bring them back from the edge into reality. Don't tell your eighteen month old not play in the puddle he's loving because other parents won't let their kids play. That is their choice, not yours. Do continue helping your ten year old make choices when he needs help. You are teaching him life skills. Don't let scoffers influence your choice to let your very mature twelve year old read murder mysteries and babysit. She has proven herself capable of making judgments about safety and well-being many times. Do empower your three year old to choose her clothes and dress herself whether the outfit matches or not. She chose alone, and that is cause for celebration.

Now that we know we are going parent our children how we see fit, let's talk about the battles nearly all parents face. Which color cup will make Betty cry today? Where *did* the favorite pair of shoes go? (They are the *only* ones Billy will wear so we've been barefoot for a week.) Oops. You put onion in dinner again. Bobby cannot fall asleep tonight because he left his cuddle blanket at daycare (or at Grandma's, his best friend's, or the car in the shop). You finally found a pair of shorts Kayla will wear and the only store within an hour of you ran out. It is homework time in the battle cage: *who will win tonight?*

I am sure all of you reading this could add your own unique battle to this list. Here is the solution: pick which ones are really worth fighting. If Betty *always* wants a yellow cup, then try to buy several yellow cups. She will still be successful if she only ever wants a yellow cup and cups won't come up on college, trade school, or job applications. Shoes. Another battle probably not worth fighting. Try to buy a few pairs in a few sizes so you don't run out. Ensure a central location for shoes so they aren't lost. Little Carol can pick the onion out of dinner or make herself a sandwich. Then she can help you remember to leave some out before adding the onion. Picture lists of the getting-out-the-door necessities can be very helpful to many people. Doing several tasks the night before can also shave off time in the morning. If we know Xander needs some relaxing brain prep time in the morning, let's be sure his alarm is set to help him get up early enough. Again, having several of the favorite element can curb this inability to perform tasks due to lack of favorite item. Have backup blankets so they can be washed too. See if the store will order you the shorts Kayla will wear. Shout out to friends who might have found similar shorts and see about sharing secrets.

And homework. These children have been in school all day then come home and are supposed to do more. Homework is insanity. However, it is also reality. If nightly homework is too much, see if the teacher can agree to a few times each week to turn in rather than everything every night. Set aside some time on Saturday and Sunday to plow away at some of the bigger pieces. Set up a schedule for after school with your child so they feel heard. Save chores for the weekend so weeknights can be freer. Build in time to be a kid too in the afternoons. Nothing sucks away childhood like schoolwork, especially when needlessly repetitive because you already know it. I know my kids would rail against repeating concepts they learned in school that day.

With the constant changes all kids go through coupled with the intensity of change neurodivergent children experience, it may seem impossible to figure out who your kids are at their core. I promise knowing them is possible. If you pay close enough attention, you will start to see their uniqueness shine through in a consistent way. Look for those little things that tend to happen in similar ways. Journal them if that helps you learn your child. You can pair circumstances with reactions from your child and from yourself along with the results of the interactions and begin to see what works and what doesn't. Many of these things will remain consistent. However, a few will evolve as your children age. But the gradual adjustments will be subtle. You can continue peeking back at the journal when things go unexpectedly and make adjustments along with your child's growth. And even if you drop something you had previously needed, you can return if you notice difficulty. For instance, Will told me he didn't need countdowns anymore when transitioning to new things, so we stopped. However, a few months later, in the midst of some other changes, he was struggling again with transitions. I asked if he needed to have countdowns again. He did. So we started them again. He has ebbed in and out of needing the reminder. These patterns are consistent themes throughout their lives and can be adjusted to easily. Being in tune with your children can lead to improved relationships overall but is particularly important with these neurodivergent children because of their more intense needs.

Life Hacks

Some of the sensory issues these kids deal with can make basic hygiene tasks a nightmare. Clearly these tasks must be completed for health and well-being. But they don't have to be as big a fight once the kids reach an age of (hopefully) being reasoned with. I can tell my one- or two year old it is time for a diaper change and try to reason with her, but I will likely have to force the issue as kindly as possible. Because one and two year olds are unreasonable. Even three and four year olds are. Sometimes around four or five (or younger or older), if we have been consistently using respectful language, we can begin to reason with these kids. I can now tell Kae, though it is unpleasant, we must brush her hair and teeth. She asks why a few times then complies. I can require Will to shower after a day at the barn because he stinks. He doesn't like to, but allowing him to choose which order and which shower is helpful. Compromising about socks in rain boots to avoid blisters instead of requiring them all the time. They are only required in rain boots and in dress shoes. I gave up the battle about underwear. My only requirement is they sit according to their clothing so no one can see up their shorts. We choose soft clothes and cut off tags. We don't wear anything stiff or rough. Haircuts are at their request only, but once we start, we finish, which requires creativity.

The following are more examples:

- Hair washing: A cup, a showerhead, under the faucet, lying down in the tub, or using a visor to keep water off the face. Try these and allow your children to choose their best method.
- Clothes: Take your child shopping, allow them to touch clothes, and decide what feels nice to them. Socks and underwear can be similar. Find them without seams!
- Toothbrushing: Sing songs, use soft brushes, use toothpaste they don't hate (they likely won't love it), and play games to help make it fun. I'm sure Pinterest has some!
- Diapers for the young ones: Using toys and signing to distract wiggly babies may help decrease diaper change woes. Changing them between activities rather than interrupting can help with the fights. Remind them of the necessity of clean pants, and unfortunately, pinning them to change quickly may be required. A diaper on backward under backward footed pajamas can help prevent the early-morning and postnap diaper removal and smear!
- Bedtime: Weighted blankets or snug sheets may help them calm their bodies and minds for sleep. A solid routine can

help too; strictness limiting more drinks, questions, and books, or a journal for the nagging questions at bedtime so they don't dwell on them, but can ask them at a more appropriate time, or a calm toy or a book in bed can greatly reduce nighttime battles.

- Toilet training boys: Seating your boys facing the tank and teaching them to tuck can greatly reduce the urine-splashed bathroom mess. There are also small, portable urinals boys can use. Allowing them to run naked in the yard can help with the sensory bit too.
- Toilet training girls: Running around naked helps here too!
- Toilet training either gender: Removing the fear surrounding the toilet is perhaps the biggest need. They've used a diaper since birth, and suddenly we change it up! We allow our toddlers and younger children into the bathroom with us as well as willing older siblings. There is no stigma surrounding the bathroom needs in our house. We talk about the process from a very young age. We use proper names for body parts and functions. We encourage them to flush when we have used the toilet, so the sound is less scary.
- Public toilets: Find the sensor for the automatic ones and cover it with a sticky note. When the child is ready, they can remove it and quickly leave the stall to avoid the noise. Or they can push the button to flush the toilet themselves. My three year old prefers this!

Notes

Resources

One of the hardest things to find can be resources. We need therapists, diagnosticians, psychologists, school support staff, sensory friendly doctors and dentists, OT, PT, speech therapists, and so much more. I cannot include a complete list, but I will do my best to highlight some starting points around the world.

Some general help for autism in the United States can be found at the following places:
- https://www.hhs.gov/programs/topic-sites/autism/autism-support/index.html
- https://www.myautism.org/what-we-do/help-hotline/
- www.autism-society.org

For anxiety:
- https://adaa.org

For giftedness in general:
- https://world-gifted.org/wcgtc-resources/gifted-support/
- https://www.nagc.org/resources-publications/resources/gifted-education-us

These tools can lead to more geographically specific resources as well. Outside the USA is a bit tougher for me to pinpoint, but here is what I have found:
- in the UK for giftedness:
  - https://www.potentialplusuk.org
  - https://www.nidirect.gov.uk/articles/supporting-gifted-and-talented-children
  - https://www.goodschoolsguide.co.uk/choosing-a-school/educating-the-gifted-child

- UK for anxiety:
  - https://www.anxietyuk.org.uk

- UK for autism:
  - https://as-uk.org
  - https://www.childautism.org.uk
  - https://www.autism.org.uk

- in Europe at large for autism:
  - https://www.autismeurope.org
  - https://act.autismeurope.org/faq

- Europe for giftedness:
  - https://www.researchgate.net/publication/282133674_GIFTED_EDUCATION_IN_VARIOUS_COUNTRIES_OF_EUROPE
  - https://www.echa.info/high-ability-in-europe/content/3-information-on-echa

- resources in Japan for autism:
  - https://savvytokyo.com/special-needs-education-japan/

- giftedness in Japan:
    - https://sk.sagepub.com/reference/giftedness/n220.xml

- Chinese information for autism:
    - http://www.autismsupportnetwork.com/news/chinese-organization-offers-hope-families-struggling-autism-8876263

- giftedness in China:
    - https://www.cogentoa.com/article/10.1080/2331186X.2017.1364881.pdf

- autism in Australia:
    - https://www.autismawareness.com.au/resources-01/educational-resources/

- giftedness in Australia:
    - https://australiangiftedsupport.com
    - http://www.aaegt.net.au
    - https://www.australiancurriculum.edu.au/resources/student-diversity/gifted-and-talented-students/

- gifted resources in Russia:
    - https://cogentoa.com/article/10.1080/2331186X.2017.1364898

- autism resources in Africa:
    - http://www.panafricancongressonautism.org
    - https://www.ernieelscentre4autism.co.za

In addition to these sources, Facebook is a treasure trove of parents throughout the world who struggle with these and many other diagnoses. A simple search of a diagnosis is bound to turn up several options. I was unable to find information on autism in Russia, and a few other resources are less helpful. But the Facebook groups are full of parents from around the globe who are waiting to support other families embarking on the journey!

Notes

Works Cited

Cherry, Kendra. "The Four Stages of Sleep (NREM and REM Sleep Cycles)." VeryWellHealth.com. https://www.verywellhealth.com/the-four-stages-o f-sleep-2795920?_ga=2.144407221.1253137745.1548117366- 1566229980.1548117354.

Gawel, Joseph. "Herzberg's Theory of Motivation and Maslow's Hierarchy of Needs." Scholarworks.umass.edu. https://scholarworks.umass.edu/pare/vol5/iss1/11/.

Huitt, W., and J. Hummel. "Piaget's Theory of Cognitive Development." Newriver.edu. https://intranet.newriver.edu/images/stories/library/ Stennett_Psychology_Articles/Piagets Theory of Cognitive Development.pdf.

Lovecky, D. V. "Hidden Gifted Learner: The Exceptionally Gifted Child." Davidsongifted.org. http://www.davidsongifted.org/search-database/entry/a10130.

McCleod, S. A. "Maslow's Hierarchy of Needs." Highgatecounselling.org. http://highgatecounselling.org.uk/members/certificate/CT2 Paper 1.pdf.

McLeod, Saul. "Edward Thorndike: The Law of Effect." Simplypsychology.org. https://www.simplypsychology.org/edward-thorndike.html.

Rueve, Marie, and Randon Welton. "Violence and Mental Illness." NCBI.gov. https://www.ncbi.nlm.nih.gov/pmc/articles/PMC2686644/.

"Medications for Anxiety." Drugs.com. https://www.drugs.com/condition/anxiety.html?category_id=&include_rx=true&include_otc=true&show_off_label=true&submitted=true.